Her Future Wars and Final Peace

LONNIE SHIPMAN

All scripture references are from the King James Version unless otherwise stated.

ISRAEL IN CRISIS
© 2024 by Lonnie Shipman
Grand Prairie, Texas

All rights reserved. We encourage the use of this material; however, in order to protect the contents from changes, neither this book, nor any part thereof, may be reprinted in any form without written permission from the publisher, except for brief excerpts used in magazine reviews, etc.

Final editing by Lise Cutshaw. Cover by GInny Tallent. Layout design by Christi Killian.

Printed in the United States of America

Published by:

Beacon Street Press
PO Box 835
Bluff City, TN 37618

ISBN 978-1-964785-12-7

Other Books by the Author

*Secrets of Prophecy Revealed:
Keys to the Second Coming of Jesus*

*Heaven's Orchestra:
The Stars Sing Praise to God*

*Treasure and the Coming Temple of God:
Finding the Ark and the Ashes*

*King of Books:
The Bible in History and Archaeology*

CONTENTS

Endorsements 7
Dedication 11
Foreword 13
Preface 15
Introduction 17
The Importance of Israel 19
The Jewish People and Their Faith 35
The Wonder of the Jewish People 53
The Possible Israel War of Psalm 83 81
The Possible Israeli War with Iran 97
The Possible Israeli War with Syria 107
The Participants of the Gog and Magog War 121
The Plan of the Gog and Magog War 137
World War I of the Tribulation 165
Additional Tribulation Wars 181
The Campaign of Armageddon 199
The Future Kingdom of God 215
Epilogue 239
Bibliography 245
About the Author 247

ENDORSEMENTS

Lonnie Shipman never ceases to amaze me! I have never seen anyone who can write so clearly about difficult subjects with such depth of research, devotion to Jesus Christ, and clear guidance for the beginning of the end times.

In this volume, *Israel in Crisis*, Dr. Shipman vividly describes future conflicts that will occur with Israel before the Lord returns for His saints. He deals with the Israel/Hamas war and other wars in a remarkable way and shows how these wars are accelerating to the end of the ages. Read and be blessed, challenged, and more devoted to our Lord.

— Dr. Jimmy Draper
President Emeritus — Lifeway

Lonnie Shipman has written an up-to-date book dealing with Israel's place in Bible prophecy. He provides current issues relating to the modern State of Israel as history appears on the verge of the Tribulation period, in which the focus centers on the modern State of Israel.

Iran often declares Israel will soon be wiped off the map, but Shipman details the trek for God's elect nation, which ultimately results in the salvation of the nation and, finally, their central place during Christ's Millennial Kingdom.

This work is a well-informed display of both the biblical text and contemporary events that will further anyone's understanding of this central issue in God's plan for history. I highly recommend *Israel in Crisis!*

— Dr. Tommy Ice
Executive Director
The Pre-Trib Research Center

Author Lonnie Shipman has distilled the essence of history's most important nation, the nation of Israel, her resurrection from the past, her continuing crisis in the present, and her prophetic promises for the future. The unmasked truth — no holds barred.

To know Israel is to know the "friend" of God. And to know Israel is to know the heart of God.

Dr. Shipman has monitored the pulse of the most important — and the most controversial — nation on Earth and has found that her heart is still beating. And she will exist as long as time can be measured.

The purpose for Israel is an eternal purpose, chosen before the foundation of the world — and destined to last forever. To destroy Israel would be to destroy the Eternal Purpose of God Himself. There she stands! And she will last as long as God Himself.

This comprehensive treatise is a *"**must read**"* for all who love Jerusalem, the "Apple of God's Eye."

— **Dr. Carl Baugh**
Founder and President
The Creation Evidence Museum of Texas
Glenrose, Texas

As the world rapidly approaches the last days, there is still so much misperception concerning the events that should take place during the Tribulation. Many end-time scholars have shared their opinions, and there is still so much to be known to decipher the prophetic mysteries found in the Scriptures. However, as a fresh approach to this defying subject, there is a new beacon shining some additional light amid the prevalent interpretative darkness still present in our days.

Dr. Lonnie Shipman's *Israel in Crisis: Her Future Wars and Final Peace* offers a biblical perspective that analyzes the scriptural evidence concerning the approaching torment over Israel. He also quotes some of the most qualified interpreters who can identify the roaring sounds of a thundering hurricane.

After carefully reading the content of his book, I conclude that Dr. Shipman's proposal is indeed an asset in clearing up the end-time controversy that has confused so many Bible believers around the world.

— **Dr. Joseph Barboza**
Professor, Louisiana Baptist University,
Shreveport, Louisiana
Senior Pastor, Hispanic Baptist Church
(Iglesia Bautista Cristiana),
Nacogdoches, Texas

With the recent rise of antisemitism on university campuses throughout America and around the world, Dr. Lonnie Shipman's work, *Israel in Crisis: Her Future Wars and Final Peace* has provided us with an invaluable, comprehensive overview of Israel's history. This book shows its vital significance in God's eternal plan, its incredible impact from Jewish people in the fields of technology, medicine, and science, and its strategic role in coming end-time events as described in Bible prophecy.

Shipman's detailed description of Israel's land and people in the coming Tribulation period, followed by Messiah's future Millennial Kingdom when peace will finally be a reality is an invaluable resource for pastors, Bible scholars, laymen, and political leaders. I recommend it without reservation.

— **Dr. David R. Nicholas, M.S., Th. M., Th. D.**
President, Professor of Theology and Apologetics,
Shasta Bible College and Graduate School,
Redding, California

DEDICATION

*This book is dedicated to the Jewish people
for whom God has a special love,*

*It is dedicated to the many servants of God and friends
who have worked to reach the Jewish people with the
gospel such as Arno Fruchtenbaum, Zola Levitt,
Charles Halff, Arno Froesne, Renald Showers,
and many more,*

*And this book is dedicated to my brother
Ronald W. Shipman,
a faithful servant of God who as a dedicated church
member has served in almost every area of church work,
from being a pastor's son, a Sunday school teacher,
a church deacon, treasurer, leader, and music minister,
as well as traveling many years in evangelism,
and whose impact for Christ is a light to
all who know him and
a good example to other believers.*

FOREWORD

I have known Dr. Lonnie Shipman for over twenty years, and he is a serious, solid student of God's Word, especially in dealing with end-time prophecy.

His timely, thorough book, *Israel in Crisis: Her Future Wars and Final Peace*, will help you understand what lies ahead for Israel and the nations. The in-depth study of Israel and future wars will explain how the world stage for future events is being set right before our eyes.

This book will enlighten your mind, encourage your heart, and expand your sense of urgency to live for our Savior as we await the sound of the trumpet.

— **Dr. Mark Hitchcock**
Senior Pastor, Faith Bible Church, Edmond, Oklahoma
Research Professor of Bible Exposition,
Dallas Theological Seminary, Dallas, Texas

PREFACE

The state of Israel since its establishment as a State has been one of crisis. Its existence has never been accepted — and never will be accepted — by the world, and this crisis will continue to be one of conflict until its Messiah comes and culminates its wars and brings His Kingdom.

Dr. Shipman has given us an exhaustive survey with a thorough explanation of the possible prophetic scenarios concerning Israel's future wars and final peace. For those asking the crucial question today of "What happens next with Israel?" this book will provide the answer!

— **Dr. Randall Price**
President, World of the Bible Ministries
Retired Professor, Liberty University
Lynchburg, Virginia

INTRODUCTION

In light of the many atrocities that have been committed against the Jewish people, such as the unprovoked attack and murder of about twelve hundred innocent Jewish people on October 7, 2023, and the subsequent invasion, attack, and routing of the terrorist group, Hamas, in the Gaza Strip, questions are often asked about details of Middle East conflicts mentioned in the Bible.

This includes questions such as "Why is there conflict between the Jews and Arabs?" "When did this conflict begin in history?" "What are the future wars of Israel mentioned in the Bible?" and "Will there ever be a time of real final peace for Israel?"

There are answers to these and many other questions about Israel's future given in the Bible. While every conflict, attack, and even possible future war that Israel might experience may not be mentioned in the Bible, all of the important wars of the end times are given in the prophetic Word.

This would include the wars near and during the Tribulation, as well as the war at the end of the Tribulation period. The Tribulation will be a time called in the Old Testament, the Time of Jacob's Trouble, (or a time when Israel is troubled), and this was prophesied as the world's most intense time of war, famine, pestilence, disease, and death for people to ever experience as God judges the world.

This time will be accompanied by many other events such as great earthquakes, five blackouts of the entire Earth's surface, hail stones falling from the sky weighing between fifteen and one hundred twenty pounds, a great meteor or asteroid also falling to Earth in destruction, the darkening of the sun, the moon turning to blood, and many other supernatural, as well as man-made disasters as God's wrath is poured out upon the Earth.

This book will also give an insight into the biblical covenants God has made with the Jews, for their promise of a Messiah who would be Savior and King, for their future in the Tribulation period, and their later time of blessing during the glorious kingdom of God on Earth.

We will see the future of each Middle Eastern nation mentioned in the Bible and look at their relationship to Israel. This book will examine each nation of the prophetic future as well as show the final blessings of Israel in the Millennial Kingdom.

Israel is often mentioned as God's timepiece for the world because each major prophecy of the world's future involves the nation of Israel and the Jewish people. God has a plan for the future, and it is centered on His chosen people.

Yet, as the Bible tells of blessings for the Jewish people, it also details unimaginable tragedies and conflicts for Israel, especially in the prophetic future. Today, there is continual growing conflict among the nations of the world and a new rise of antisemitism in America and Europe.

There are dangers of war with Israel from each of the Middle East nations and the constant threat of terrorism, especially from the followers of Islam. In recent days, there has been a growing threat from Iran and Syria and war seems to loom on the horizon. In light of these rising dangers and the unending terrorism and hatred, what is the fate of Israel? Where can Israel turn? Is there any hope for the future of Israel?

CHAPTER ONE

THE IMPORTANCE OF ISRAEL

While being surrounded by enemy nations on all sides with only limited relationships, and continuing to experience rampant antisemitism around the world, Israel has few friends, and the Jewish people have few places of refuge. But despite experiencing a long history of persecution and racism, Israel has a friend in the United States of America.

America has steadfastly stood with Israel, especially during past conflicts like the Yom Kippur War. In spite of the recent rise of renewed antisemitism in America from many people in liberal circles, in the socialist agenda of many liberal American universities, and in part because of the huge influx of immigrants to America, especially of recent illegal entry, American policy and the American people still stand solidly with Israel.

America Is a Friend to Israel

While being interviewed by one of America's leading news reporters on "Nightline," correspondent Ted Koppel asked former American President Richard Nixon, "You make the observation in your book, and you have said it many times that no president will ever desert Israel." President Nixon responded, "Correct. I put it more bluntly. As I told congressional leaders during the 1973 Yom Kippur War, no American president will let Israel go down the tubes, Democrat or Republican, it is not an issue."

Koppel asks, "All right, that is stated fairly categorically. Yet, in your book, you make it clear, at the same time, that Israel is really of not any enormous strategic value to the United States anymore." Nixon again responds, "That is correct."

Koppel then asks, "All right. So, why then would the United States continue to burden itself with huge loans, in some cases outright grants, and jeopardize possibly young American fighting men, when there is no strategic value involved?"

Nixon states, "Because the United States is concerned with more than strategic values. That is maybe a weakness but that is the way we are. And there are moral issues involved here. We do not have an alliance with Israel, as you know. They are not an ally of the United States in the technical sense.

"But we have a bond to Israel that is much stronger. It is a moral commitment, because of what happened during the Holocaust and a moral commitment because it is a democracy, the only democracy in that area. And under the circumstances, that is why American presidents and the American people in the future will support, all out, the survival of Israel if it is attacked."

Koppell then says, "You have always been a very tough, pragmatic man. And I just wonder, if you were the president of Israel and you heard Richard Nixon talking that way, or for that matter, you heard any sitting American president talk that way, and say that there is really no strategic value anymore, how much faith would you place in that kind of moral commitment if push really came to shove?"

Nixon again responds, "If I were the president of Israel, I would put a great deal of faith in it because of the track record of the United States, and also because he would know that that is the way the American people are. There is no doubt whatever of our commitment to Israel." [1]

Yet, Israel has an even stronger friend and supporter who will always be there to help Israel, because God is on

---

1. Archive of The Richard Nixon Foundation, "Nightline" interview, January 7, 1992. Accessed on February 24, 2024. https://nixonfoundation.org

her side. Through all of the stupendous events of persecution and war, we continue to see God's special love and protection of Israel.

Israel's Special Place in God's Plan and Heart

Israel has always held a special place in God's plan and His heart. And Israel was chosen by God to be His special people as an act of the grace of God. After God had dealt with mankind as a group, through the time of Adam and Eve, Noah and the Flood, and the time of the Tower of Babel, God then chose to show His mercy, grace, and great love to one man who would grow into a family and eventually the great nation of Israel.

The earlier part of Genesis covered about two thousand years of human history and the rest of the Old and New Testament covers only a little more than two thousand years, but here God shows great detail in demonstrating how He reveals Himself to man. In grace and mercy, He deals with His chosen people, using them to bring about the coming of the Savior and the recording of the Word of God and to be an example and witness to the Gentile nations of God and His care for mankind.

Abraham

God chose the man Abraham in the Ur of the Chaldees to show His great love for man. Abraham was first named Abram, meaning *father*, and he descended from the sons of Shem through an earlier grandfather named ***Eber***, meaning ***crosser*** from which we get the name ***Hebrew***. This designation may have been given to the Hebrew people because they crossed the Euphrates River.

During this period, the Bible scholar William Scroggie reminds us, "After the ***world*** had turned from God, He left it and chose a ***man*** through whom He would ultimately, through Christ, reach the lost ***world***."[2] God chose to bless Abraham and his future people with promises and God also planned a series of biblical covenants to show the extent of His blessing to the Jewish people.

The city of Ur, near Babylon, had become the center of worship of the celestial bodies of the skies, especially the moon, foreshadowing the beginnings of the religion of Islam which also has its roots in the worship of the moon. Islam's founder, the false prophet Mohammed, was a pagan priest of moon worship before he founded Islam. The city's name of Ur comes from the name of the moon god, Hur or Hurki.[3] Into this place of idolatry, God came and spoke to Abram.

> *Now the* LORD *had said unto Abram, Get thee out of thy country, and from thy kindred, and from thy father's house, unto a land that I will shew thee: And I will make of thee a great nation, and I will bless thee, and make thy name great; and thou shalt be a blessing: And I will bless them that bless thee, and curse him that curseth thee: and in thee shall all families of the earth be blessed.*
> — Genesis 12:1–3

The Promise to Abraham

God called him to leave his kindred family, and to leave his homeland, and to journey to a ***land*** God would show him. The Lord promised to make him a great ***nation***, to bless him and make his name great, and to make him a ***blessing*** to others. There is the Promise of a ***land***, of a great ***nation***, and that Abram would be a great ***blessing***. This blessing is a reference to the Messiah who would come from the line of Abraham.

This is the beginning of a new dispensation or period

---

2. William Scroggie, *The Unfolding Drama of Redemption* (Kregel Classics, 1995), p. 99.
3. Moon Lore: *Moon Worship: III The Moon a Worldwide Deity*, https://sacredtexts.com

called the Dispensation of Promise. During this time, God is working with mankind through Abraham and his descendants. They were told to follow God, and Abraham and his descendants began to make altars to the Lord. The Jews were told to believe in God by faith, to perpetuate their line, and to possess the land. However, they eventually failed God in possessing the land, they intermarried with Gentiles, and they were judged by slavery in Egypt.

God has blessed the Jewish people in a very special way in preserving the Jewish people as a **nation** and even brought them back to their homeland. God used the Jewish people to bring about the Holy Scriptures, the Word of God, and to bring about Jesus Christ, the Son of God. The entire world has also had the **blessing** of God through Abraham by his descendant Jesus Christ who has blessed all people of the world by providing eternal salvation in Heaven through believing in the Savior. Even today, God is at work with events in the Middle East, restoring the **land** fully to the nation of Israel.

The Abrahamic Covenant

When Abram heard from God, he did not follow the Lord completely by leaving his father and kindred to go to a land that God would show him, but he went to Haran and took his father and his nephew who were some of his kindred. After his father died, Abram continued to the land of Canaan. When he arrived in the land, God appeared to him again and gave him the Abrahamic Covenant.

A covenant is an ancient and very strong binding agreement two people would make in the Old Testament times and they would seal this covenant in the blood of an animal. After slaying the animal, the two people would walk between the two parts as their sealing and signing of this binding agreement. While people may make a promise or commitment, a covenant is considered a much stronger agreement to keep.

The Types of Covenants

A covenant can be conditional or unconditional, meaning breakable or unbreakable. The difference in the two kinds of biblical covenants is seen in their statement of promise: *conditional*, depending upon man using the "If ye will obey" formula of Exodus 19:5, and **unconditional**, depending upon God using the "I will" formula of Genesis 9:11.

A **conditional** covenant is binding on both parties for its fulfillment, that is, the response of the one making the covenant is conditioned by the response of the party with whom the covenant was made. Conversely, an unconditional covenant is only binding on the one who makes the covenant, although blessings may require a response for the blessing.[4]

God put Abram to sleep, and He alone walked between the two animal parts, making this an unconditional covenant. God guaranteed the keeping of the Abrahamic Covenant, thus it is unbreakable and stands on God's Word. All of the biblical covenants are unconditional except the Mosaic Covenant when God gave the law and He told the Jewish people of blessings and cursings based upon their faithfulness in keeping the law.

Notice that all biblical covenants are literal, eternal, depend entirely upon the integrity of God, and are made with the covenant people of Israel. The Mosaic Covenant followed these guidelines, but it was the only temporary covenant.

---

[4]. Rick Bowman, "The Covenants," *The Dictionary of Premillennial Theology* (Grand Rapids, MI: Kregel Press, 1995), pp. 72–73.

The Covenant of Faith

God had given Abraham the promise of a new land, of a new family which would become a great nation and to make him a blessing in Genesis 12. Next, in Genesis 15, when Abraham was eighty-five, God gave him the covenant of faith that God alone made, and Abraham believed God and was justified. This part of the covenant emphasized faith in God as the basis for salvation.

Then the sign of the covenant was given to Abraham and his male household about thirteen years later in Genesis 17 when they were commanded to be circumcised. Thus, salvation was not through circumcision but through faith, and the sign of circumcision was an outward sign of acceptance, similar to putting a seal on a contract and symbolic in the sense of the church's use of believer's baptism, to show their faith in God to others. Circumcision was not needed or effectual in salvation, as Paul tells us in Romans and Galatians, but was a sign of one's personal faith in God.

The Land Boundary of the Abrahamic Covenant

God told Abraham to walk the land and of all the land he saw, that land he would also possess. God told Abraham the extent of the land's boundaries in Genesis 15:12–21. The borders of the land are to extend from the Euphrates River in the north and the land of the Hittites to the River of Egypt in the south. Although the northern boundary seems clear, there has been confusion about the southern boundary.

While some people have surmised that the River of Egypt is the Nile River, from various biblical passages we know that this actually refers to one of the fingers of the Nile River, roughly corresponding to the most eastern branch at the line of the modern Suez Canal. There is also a Brook of Egypt which was mentioned by some of the prophets as the southern boundary of Jewish settlement.

So, the people will live in Israel as far south as the Brook of Egypt (the Wadi-el-Arish), an area in the central Sinai Peninsula. And they will possess the land unto the boundary of the area of the modern Suez Canal, called the River of Egypt.[5]

Yet, Abraham never possessed the entire land in his lifetime but only a small portion of the land; he even paid money for a burial place. Consequently, Abraham will be resurrected for the time of the Millennial Kingdom when he will possess all the promises of God. And the boundaries of Israel will be fulfilled and completely possessed in the Millennial Kingdom.

The Continuing of the Abrahamic Covenant

God then renewed the Abrahamic Covenant with Isaac and with Jacob, showing that He was guaranteeing the promises and blessings through the Jewish line of people. And they will also be resurrected for the full benefit of the promises. The full possession of the land will happen at the beginning of the Millennium. The world will be ruled from Israel and Jerusalem will be her capital and the capital of the world, where Jesus will reign as Messiah King as well as King of Kings and Lord of all Lords.

There were several covenants given to the Jewish people which are still active promises of God. If God did not fulfill these promises, He would not be trustworthy, but God cannot lie, as one of the covenants reminds us.

Thus, all the promises made to the Jewish people must be fulfilled with the Jewish people, and not by replacement people such as Replacement Theology teaches. The church will never rule a kingdom for God, but there must

---

5. Arnold Fruchtenbaum, *The Footsteps of Messiah: A Study of the Sequence of Prophetic Events* (Tustin, CA: Ariel Ministries Press, 1983), pp. 301–302.

be a literal future Millennial Kingdom for Israel, else God's numerous promises to Israel throughout the Old Testament would not be true.

The Coming Redeemer

There must be a coming Messiah to be the Suffering Servant of Isaiah 53 who was wounded for our transgressions and bruised for our iniquities. This is the prophecy of a coming Savior who would die for the sins of the world. Jesus fulfilled this prophecy by dying on the cross, bearing the sins of the world, and paying the world's sin debt, and He rose from the grave to prove that He is God in the flesh and the victor over death.

Also, there must be a Messiah king of Isaiah 9 who is the Wonderful, Counselor, the Mighty God [God incarnate or God in the flesh], the Everlasting Father [literally the eternal God on earth], and the Prince of Peace. And this Messiah king will sit and rule upon the throne of His father, David.

This was first verified with the promise given to Mary that *"He shall be great, and shall be called the Son of the Highest: and the Lord God shall give unto him the throne of his father David"* (Luke 1:32). And this promise will be later fulfilled by the coming of Jesus to rule in majesty over the world for a literal thousand years of peace on Earth.

The future fulfillment of the Abrahamic Covenant is described in many passages of Scripture. Leviticus 26:40–45 tells us that following the national regeneration of Israel, they will be restored and possess the land that has long lay desolate. Isaiah 27:12 tells us that Israel will then possess all of this land for the first time in her history.

The Abrahamic Covenant has several provisions, but there are three primary aspects: the promise of the land, the seed, and the blessing. The land aspect is further developed in the Land Covenant (sometimes called the

Palestinian Covenant). The seed aspect is further developed in the Davidic Covenant, and the blessing aspect is further developed in the New Covenant. The Abrahamic Covenant is progressive, and these successive covenants are sometimes seen as sub-covenants or as a progressive fulfillment of the Abrahamic Covenant.

The Mosaic Covenant

The Mosaic Covenant was given to Moses and the Jewish people in Exodus 20:1-32:18 and was broken almost immediately by Exodus 32:15-29. It was a constitution for the nation of Israel and instituted a sacrificial system of worship with a Tabernacle (later continued in the Temple) and the giving of the law.

This included a priesthood and the giving of six hundred thirteen laws to lead the people to follow righteousness and to show their need for God and His holiness, mercy, and grace. This was a conditional covenant with God promising blessings and cursings depending on the faithfulness of His people.

The Meaning of the Law

The law was given as a standard of righteousness, to expose and identify sin, and to reveal God's holiness. The law was given after the Abrahamic Covenant. Although the way to God was still through faith, the Mosaic law was added to expose sin, and Israel's and mankind's need for salvation by God as established by Genesis 3:15. The promise to Abraham was and still is in effect.

Because the law was used by many Jewish people as access to God (as some substituted their sacrificial works for faith), it became a curse that enslaved the people to works without faith in God. But Christ came to remove the curse of the law. *"Christ hath redeemed us from the curse of the law ... That the blessing of Abraham might come on the Gentiles through Jesus Christ; that we might receive the promise of the Spirit through faith"* (Galatians 3:13-14).

To Reveal the Holiness of God

The purpose of the law was not given as a means of salvation because salvation is always by grace through faith (Rom. 3:20, 28; Gal. 2:16, 3:11, 21). The law was given to reveal the holiness of God, and the standard of righteousness demanded by God for a proper relationship (Lev. 19:1-2; 37; 11:44; 1 Pet. 1:15-16) and was described as holy, righteous, and good (Rom. 7:12). It was to provide a rule of conduct for Old Testament saints (Lev. 11:44-45; 19:2; 20:7-8, 26).

To Institute Organized Worship

The law was given to provide individual and corporate worship, such as the seven seasons of worship for the Jewish people (Lev. 23). The law was given to keep the Jews a distinct people in worship, eating habits, clothing laws, and various smaller details (Lev. 11:44-45; Deut. 7:6; 14:1-2).

To Make a Distinction for the Jewish People

The law was a middle wall of partition separating Gentiles from Jewish people and the Gentiles could not enjoy the blessings unless they lived as Jews under the law. Thus, living under the law made a distinction for the Jewish people.

To Reveal Sin in Mankind

The law was given to reveal sin (Rom. 3:19-20; 5:20; 7:7). The law then showed the sinner that there was nothing that he could do to please God, that he could not keep the law perfectly or attain to the righteousness of the law (Rom. 7:14-25) and this would drive the sinner to faith in God (Rom. 8:1-4; Gal. 3:24-25).

To Demonstrate the Blood Sacrifice

The key element of the Mosaic Covenant was the blood sacrifice (Lev. 17:11). There were five different types of offerings (Lev. 1-7). The blood of the sacrifice only covered the sin, it did not remove it (Heb. 10:1-4).[6] The sacrifice provided forgiveness and restored fellowship with God and pictured a future complete sacrifice of the coming Lamb of God to pay for the sin of the world, which would forgive and remove sin through Christ's blood and offer redemption to all the world.

The Recording of Scripture

When the law was given, Moses wrote it down as the Book of the Covenant (Exodus 20:18-23:33) and it was the first part of Scripture ever written down (Exodus 24:4). The terms were told to the people, it was ratified with the sprinkling of blood on the altar and on the people, and the laws were civil, religious (or ceremonial), and social.

The Law Is a Schoolmaster

The Mosaic Covenant was given to be a schoolmaster to teach the people that they were sinners and that their sins must be paid for by a sacrifice. They were to look for a coming redeemer who would save the people and provide payment for the sins of the world.

The Law Was to Be Temporary

This Mosaic Covenant also was only to be temporary and

---

6. Arnold Fruchtenbaum, *Israelogy: The Missing Link in Systematic Theology*, (Tustin, CA: Ariel Ministries Press, 1989), pp. 588-593.

was to be replaced by the New Covenant prophesied in Jeremiah 31. This would be a future time when Israel would serve God by the Word of God and the Spirit of God living in their hearts. Under the New Covenant, they would live in righteousness without the requirements of the outer workings of the law.

The Land Covenant

The Land Covenant is unconditional; it was given in Deuteronomy 29:1–30:20 and it guarantees that Israel will possess the Promised Land. This covenant includes several provisions. Moses prophetically spoke of Israel's coming disobedience to the Mosaic law and their judgment and subsequent scattering all over the world (Deut. 20:2–30:1) but there will come a time in the latter days when Israel returns and possesses the Promised Land.

Then the Land Covenant expounds details of Israel's final restoration: Israel will repent (30:2), Messiah will return (30:3), Israel will be regathered (30:3–4), Israel will possess the Promised land (30:5), Israel will be regenerated (30:6), Israel's enemies will be judged (30:7), and Israel will receive all of her full blessings including the blessings of the Messianic Kingdom.[7]

The giving of the Land Covenant to Israel shows that the Mosaic Covenant did not replace the Abrahamic Covenant, and its restatement in Ezekiel 16:1–63 shows that God always loves Israel, in spite of her unfaithfulness. God punished Israel by dispersion, yet she will be regathered for a future restoration and Israel will possess the land.

The Davidic Covenant

The Davidic Covenant is unconditional, and it was given in 2 Samuel 7:4–16 and 1 Chronicles 17:3–15. It promises

---
7. Ibid., p. 582.

that David's throne, lineage, and kingdom will be eternal, and it assures the coming of the Millennial Kingdom in which Christ will reign on Earth.

David is promised an eternal house or dynasty (2 Sam. 7:22; 16:1; 1 Chron. 17:10), Solomon was to reign on David's throne (2 Sam. 7:12), Solomon would build the Temple (2 Sam. 7:13), and the throne of David's and Solomon's kingdom would be established forever (2 Sam. 7:13, 16). Solomon would be disciplined for disobedience, but God would not remove His lovingkindness (2 Sam. 7:14–15), Messiah would come from the seed of David (1 Chron. 17:11), and Messiah's throne, house, and kingdom would be established forever (1 Chron. 17:12–14).[8]

This will result in an eternal house or dynasty, an eternal throne, an eternal kingdom, and an eternal descendant, meaning Messiah would originate from David's line. This kingdom will exist for a thousand years during the Millennial reign of Christ on Earth, and the eternal aspect of the kingdom of God will continue through the future eternal state of the new Heaven and new Earth.

The New Covenant

The New Covenant is unconditional, and it will have its ultimate fulfillment in the Millennial Kingdom. It was given in Jeremiah 31:31–34 and was given to Israel because they broke and could not fulfill the Mosaic Covenant.

This covenant was made between God and both houses of Israel (or the entire Jewish nation), it was given to replace the broken Mosaic Covenant, it promises the regeneration of Israel, and salvation is the key aspect of the entire covenant (Jer. 32:33; Isa. 59:21).

This covenant tells us the regeneration of Israel will include all Jewish people (Jer. 31:34; Isa. 61:9), and there is

---

8. Ibid., pp. 584–585.

provision for forgiveness of sin (Jer. 31:34). This covenant will include the indwelling of the Holy Spirit (Jer. 31:33; Ezek. 36:27), and the sanctuary will be rebuilt (Ezek. 37:26–28) which will be the Millennial Temple.[9]

Because the Messiah Savior came to provide salvation to all who would believe, the group of believers after Jesus' first coming in redemption includes a combined Jewish and Gentile church today. Thus, the blessings aspect of the New Covenant applies to Christian believers today, but the primary aspects of the full New Covenant fulfillment will be for the Jewish people in the Millennial Kingdom.

Paul tells us in 2 Corinthians 3:5–9 that the Mosaic law engraved on stones was to bring death, but the New Covenant would be a ministry of the Spirit that would abound to righteousness and greater glory. Through the New Covenant of the Spirit living in the heart of believers, the church and Gentile believers might participate with Israel in the fulfillment of the covenants and receive blessings, especially during the Millennium.

The covenants were given exclusively to Israel as a national and ethnic people. Their full and complete fulfillment will be with Israel alone as God promised and this complete fulfillment will happen in the Millennium during the Kingdom of God on Earth as Jesus rules from Israel (Eph. 2:11–22; Rom. 11:17–24).

The Wife of Jehovah

Israel has a special relationship with God as the wife of Jehovah. Not only are the Jewish people the chosen people of God, but they have been chosen to bring about the earlier Jewish system of worship, to be the examples of faith in the Bible, to administer the recording of the Word of God, and to fulfill the coming of Messiah, who was Jesus Christ.

---
9. Ibid., pp. 586–587.

They are also called the wife of Jehovah. Ezekiel 16:1–63 tells us several illuminating details of God's special care for Israel.

God recounts His love for Israel in her infancy (Ezek. 16:1–7). Israel was chosen by God and became related to Jehovah by marriage; hence she is called the wife of Jehovah (Ezek. 16:8–14). Unfortunately, Israel played the harlot (Ezek. 16:15–34) and was then judged with the diaspora, by being scattered over all the world (Ezek. 16:35–52), but she will be regathered to the land of Israel and be given a full restoration according to the Land Covenant (Ezek. 16:53–63).

In Joshua 24, Joshua reminds Israel of God's promises to Abraham, that He delivered them through Moses, and that God helped Israel defeat her enemies and possess the land. Because they can believe God's word, Joshua tells Israel to serve the Lord alone. Israel later fell to a cycle of idolatry and repentance until God finally scattered His people. But God will bring them back in the last days.

God has never forgotten Israel. She is the apple of His eye, His special joy and crown and God will keep all of His promises and covenants with Israel, they will not be replaced or forgotten. God is coming again, and Israel will be restored and regenerated as an entire nation.

Every Jewish person will return to God at the time of the Millennial Kingdom and at that time will there never again be a Jewish person who is not a believer who is faithful to God. The entire Jewish nation will believe in the Lord Jesus Christ at the time of Armageddon and all the nation will remain faithful believers for the rest of Earth's existence during the Millennium.

CHAPTER TWO

THE JEWISH PEOPLE AND THEIR FAITH

The Jewish people developed a worship system based upon the Mosaic law with a sacrificial system of five sacrifices centered at the Temple. They also later developed the synagogue system during the Babylonian exile because they could not worship at their Temple after its destruction. And they later used both systems of worship.

The Jewish faith is one of the oldest and most fascinating forms of worship in the world. This unique worship involves sincere prayer, a diligent study of the Scriptures and adherence to God's law, beautiful and emotional music of worship, and a sacrificial system of offerings to God.

A brief comparison of the Jewish form of worship to other ancient forms of worship sets it high above all pagan religions by beauty, purity, and justice. For example, the Jewish faith was distinctively monotheistic, utilized only animal sacrifices, and emphasized a high sense of holy, moral conduct.

The Jewish Sacred Writings

Because God spoke personally to Abraham, Moses, and several early Jewish leaders, they recorded the Word of God as Scripture and this became part of their sacred writings. The Jewish faith is based upon believing and practicing their sacred writings. The Jewish writings are divided into two sections: the Scriptures and tradition.

The Scriptures

The Scriptures are called the *Tanakh*. This is an acronym for the five books of Moses, made up of the Hebrew initials for the words *Torah* (the "Written Law"), *Neveim* (the "Prophets"), and *Ketubim* (the "Writings"), from the books of the Old Testament which comprise the three divisions of the Hebrew Bible. This is equivalent to the Old Testament of the Bible.

The Torah ("teachings, learning, or law") is the name for the Pentateuch, the first five books of the Bible. The Torah, or the Written Law, which Jews believe was revealed directly by God to Moses on Mount Sinai (Exodus 20:1–32:18), lays down the fundamental laws of moral and physical conduct. But when the term is used in a wider sense, the Torah comprises all teachings of Judaism including the Hebrew Scripture, the Talmud, and any generally accepted rabbinical interpretation.

Thus, the Scripture is the Tanakh. The Tanakh = the Torah (הָרוֹת — the law) + Nevi'im (מִיאִיבָנ — the prophets) + Ketuvim (כְּמִיבוּת — the writings).

The Torat Moshe (the "Law of Moses") is the original autograph of the first five books of the Tanakh (the Old Testament). These first five books are called the Torah (Hebrew) or Pentateuch (Greek), written by Moses and deposited either inside or beside the Ark of the Covenant (Deuteronomy 31:24–26).

The Tradition

The *Tradition* is the added words given to Moses and other early leaders by tradition to help to understand and follow the Scripture. The traditions consist of the *Mishnah* and *Gemara*.

The *Mishnah* ("learning, repetition") is the earliest written collection of Jewish oral law (that is, Jewish religious and legal teaching handed down orally). It is a collection of interpretations of the legal portions of the Torah and a codification of traditional Jewish practice. The *Gemara* ("study") is the commentary material included in the Talmud from Jewish tradition, as opposed to material from the Bible of logical reasoning.

The *Talmud* ("teaching") is the entire corpus of Jewish oral law. It includes the *Mishnah* together with a written compendium of discussions and commentary on the *Mishnah* which is the *Gemara*. There are also additional Tannaitic writings from early rabbinical teachers. These teachings and rulings span a period between Ezra in the Old Testament (c. 450 BC) and the middle of the Roman period (c. AD 550).

Thus, the Tradition is the *Talmud*. The *Talmud* = the *Mishnah* (the "learning") + the *Gemara* (the "study").

Because it includes rulings made by generations of scholars and jurists in many academies in both Palestine and Babylon, it exists in two versions: the *Jerusalem* Talmud (discussions in the Jerusalem academies) and the *Babylonian* Talmud (discussions in the Babylonian academies).

Thus, the *Scriptures* given by God are the *Tanakh*, the Old Testament given supernaturally by God, and the *Traditions* are the *Talmud*, the oral traditions and commentary from the history of Judaism. Christians and Jews alike accept the Old Testament, while the Jews also base their worship and beliefs on their tradition.

Jewish Theology

Because Jewish theology is originally Bible-based, there is a similarity with part of Christian theology. Belief in the New Testament and its doctrine for Christians makes a distinction from Jews, who only follow the Old Testament. But they each believe in following the same teaching of morality and dedication to God.

During the Jewish exile to Babylon, the Jews could not follow all of their laws because about two hundred laws were connected to the Temple. After the destruction of the First Temple, the Jews developed a system of worship called Synagogue worship (Greek, "gathering together") for devotion and study of the Bible and the Talmud.

The Messianic Age

Like Christian believers, Jews are looking for an end-time series of events, and many Jews believe in a coming Messiah and messianic age.

The Jews await a messianic age or messianic era. This is the era of redemption, that period that spans the beginning of redemption for the Jewish people in the land of Israel (interpreted by some as 1948) through the coming and rule of King Messiah at the end of the six thousand years of history to bring a reign of universal peace, moral justice, and spiritual life.

The Jews call this end-time the *'Acharit ha-yamim* (סִימָיָה תִירְחאַ) — the "end of days"). This is the term used to designate that period of the end-time described by the biblical prophets. It includes *Yom YHVH* ("the day of the Lord") in which God's judgment falls upon Israel's adversaries, as well as *Yemot ha-Mashiach* ("the days of Messiah"), the period preceding the judgment. It is followed by *'olam ha-ba* ("the world to come"), the eschatological future world.

The Messiah

Jewish people are also looking for a coming Messiah and they call him **Mashiach** (the "anointed one"). Sometimes the word used for Messiah is **Moshiach** (the Ashkenazi-accented Hebrew spelling of Messiah).

The Messiah, in contemporary orthodox Judaism, is

envisioned as a human political and military leader who will usher in the Day of Redemption for the Jewish people. The term is equivalent to the Greek term *Christos* from which is derived the English term *Christ*.

In historic orthodox Christian definition, the Jewish concept of Messiah is further revealed as God the Son being sent to fulfill this role. Thus, Christians accept a divine Messiah whom they identify with the historic Jewish man, Jesus of Nazareth, and they believe in his crucifixion, death, and resurrection.

The Jewish Return to God

And the rabbis also believe in a coming spiritual awakening they call *Teshuvah* (תְּשׁוּבָה — the "turning"). This is the act or condition of spiritual repentance, that is, a turning to God from self, sin, or idols which includes practices that take preeminence over God. Prophetically, the term refers to the spiritual regeneration of the Jewish remnant (Isa. 59:20–21; Rom. 11:26–27) at the end of the Tribulation period with the coming of the Messiah (Zech. 12:10–13:2).

Ezekiel 36:23–28 tells us about this future time when Israel will return to the Lord as an entire nation.

> *And I will sanctify my great name, which was profaned among the heathen, which ye have profaned in the midst of them; and the heathen shall know that I am the LORD, saith the Lord GOD, when I shall be sanctified in you before their eyes. For I will take you from among the heathen, and gather you out of all countries, and will bring you into your own land. Then will I sprinkle clean water upon you, and ye shall be clean: from all your filthiness, and from all your idols, will I cleanse you. A new heart also will I give you, and a new spirit will I put within you: and I will take away the stony heart*

out of your flesh, and I will give you an heart of flesh. And I will put my spirit within you, and cause you to walk in my statutes, and ye shall keep my judgments, and do them. And ye shall dwell in the land that I gave to your fathers; and ye shall be my people, and I will be your God.

At this time, the entire nation will believe in the Lord. In verse 25, when God refers to sprinkling the nation with clean water, this is the purification water of the ashes of the red heifer. So, in many ways, the return of the Jews to Israel and the red heifer are vitally connected. This thinking is also connected to looking for a coming Messiah and the rebuilding of the Jewish Temple.

Israel's Return to the Land in Unbelief

One other interesting question has to do with the current faith of most of the people in Israel today. If a poll was taken, it would be found that many of the Jewish people are agnostic, and not concerned with God or any participation in organized religion. They are not necessarily against religion. It is just not a part of their life.

There are also some Jews who are only slightly involved in the Jewish faith. And only a small percentage of the people of Israel today would be orthodox Jews. Yet, does this fit the view of Israel in Bible prophecy?

Some students of the Bible have noticed that prophecies of the future Millennial Kingdom portray Israel as the key Millennial country of the world and that all of Israel at that time are believers. Yet, this does not fit modern Israel, so some people have doubted the Bible's prophecies.

The Two Jewish Returns to the Land of Israel

Yet, they do not realize that the Bible mentions two returns of the Jews to the land of Israel, one in unbelief and the second return in faith.

In Ezekiel 20:33-38, the Bible tells us that Israel will return in a state of unbelief before a time of judgment. Here Ezekiel writes,

> *As I live, saith the Lord GOD, surely with a mighty hand, and with a stretched out arm, and with fury poured out, will I rule over you: And I will bring you out from the people, and will gather you out of the countries wherein ye are scattered, with a mighty hand, and with a stretched out arm, and with fury poured out. And I will bring you into the wilderness of the people, and there will I plead with you face to face. Like as I pleaded with your fathers in the wilderness of the land of Egypt, so will I plead with you, saith the Lord GOD. And I will cause you to pass under the rod, and I will bring you into the bond of the covenant: And I will purge out from among you the rebels, and them that transgress against me: I will bring them forth out of the country where they sojourn, and they shall not enter into the land of Israel: and ye shall know that I am the LORD.*

In this passage, Ezekiel compares this return to the time of Israel's wilderness wanderings. During the wanderings, Israel rejected the report of the two spies who gave a good report. Because of their lack of faith in taking Canaan, an entire generation wandered in the wilderness until all but the two spies had died and a new generation took the land. Israel left Egypt as former slaves but entered Canaan as free men to take the land.

This first regathering is in unbelief as is described in the repeated phrase *"with a mighty hand, and with a stretched out arm, and with fury poured out."* This regathering tells of a time of regathering after God's wrath had been poured out, such as the Jew's many persecutions and the Holocaust, and the rebels will be purged during the future judgment of the Tribulation.

Yet, the first regathering happens before the day of the Lord's fierce anger, or before the day of judgment in the Tribulation. Zephaniah 2:1–2 says,

> *Gather yourselves together, yea, gather together, O nation not desired; Before the decree bring forth, before the day pass as the chaff, before the fierce anger of the LORD come upon you, before the day of the LORD's anger come upon you.*

Ezekiel 22:17–22 tells of Israel being tried and purged through a refiner's fire as silver, iron, brass, and tin to cleanse the people of the dross or rebellions. Also, in Ezekiel 36:22–24, God tells them that the regathering takes place before the regeneration.

Israel's Return to God as a Nation

The Bible clearly tells of a second return to the land when all of Israel has faith in God. This second regathering in faith is foretold in Isaiah 11:9–12.

> *They shall not hurt nor destroy in all my holy mountain: for the earth shall be full of the knowledge of the LORD, as the waters cover the sea. And in that day there shall be a root of Jesse, which shall stand for an ensign of the people; to it shall the Gentiles seek: and his rest shall be glorious. And it shall come to pass in that day, that* **the Lord shall set his hand again the second time to recover the remnant of his people,** *which shall be left, from Assyria, and from Egypt, and from Pathros, and from Cush, and from Elam, and*

from Shinar, and from Hamath, and from the islands of the sea. And he shall set up an ensign for the nations, and shall assemble the outcasts of Israel, and gather together the dispersed of Judah from the four corners of the earth [emphasis added].

At this Millennial Kingdom time, all people, Jew and Gentile, will have returned in faith to God, so this is a second regathering in belief. The unbelieving Gentiles would have been killed in Armageddon and judged; only believers of Jews and Gentiles will enter the Millennial Kingdom.

Israel will be the location and focus of God's worship and the people will serve the Lord together in united faith. The people will worship God in the Temple of Jerusalem and the Jews are regathered from around the world in faith.

Thus, Israel has gathered today in unbelief awaiting the Lord's fierce anger in the Tribulation, but God will have mercy and save His people at Armageddon. After they have been tried in a furnace of fire, they will return the second time to God in faith as God establishes a kingdom of righteousness and the knowledge of the Lord surrounds the whole Earth, as the waters of the sea cover the world.

The Promise of a Coming Messiah

After the sin of Adam and Eve, taking the forbidden fruit in the Garden of Eden, mankind was forbidden to eat from the Tree of Life, banished from the Garden, and judged with death for their sin. This death was gradual physical death and spiritual death, including separation from God, judgment, and eternal punishment.

But God promised a way to be saved from this judgment. He showed them redemption pictured through the sacrifice of a lamb to cover their sins like the skins of a slain animal covered their nakedness in the Garden.

Mankind knew of Satan's temptation to sin by the Garden experience, and man, woman, the snake, and the Earth were all judged. But man was promised a future redemption.

In Genesis 3:15, God said, *"And I will put enmity between thee and the woman, and between thy seed and her seed; it shall bruise thy head, and thou shalt bruise his heel."*

The Seed of a Woman

This was the promise of a "seed" from the woman that would be able to overcome sin and its consequences. It was pictured in the sacrifice of the lamb, first mentioned to be offered by Abel. Later, the lamb was the primary sacrifice of the Jewish system of worship under the Mosaic law.

After mankind's earlier sinful state was judged by the flood, and his sinful rebellion reappeared in the rebellion of the tower of Babel, God then chose to use the Jewish people as His chosen representative, both in faith and service.

God chose Abraham to begin the seed which would be a family that grew to become a nation. He promised him the Abrahamic Covenant, which included the promise of coming to God by faith, as well as the promise of a seed, land, and blessing to all the Earth.

This promise continued through the line of Isaac, and Jacob, and the sons of Jacob became the twelve tribes of Israel. Here, the promise of a leader moved to the line of Judah, for Jacob prophesied, *"The sceptre shall not depart from Judah, nor a lawgiver from between his feet, until Shiloh come; and unto him shall the gathering of the people be"* (Gen. 49:10).

The Coming Political Leader

From this prophecy in Genesis 49:10, the people knew that there would come a man who would be the political leader of the people. As God continued to reveal Himself to man, there was also a continual revealing of the future and the nature and identity of the coming leader.

God spoke to Moses in the burning bush; Moses received the law at Mount Sinai and prophesied a deliverer for his people. This view of a political leader from Judah as well as a spiritual redeemer for mankind is gradually developed into the concept of the Messiah as more revelation by God is given through Scripture.

The Coming Spiritual Leader

Just as priests and kings were anointed with oil for their special duties, the Messiah is "the Anointed One," and He was anointed by God and covered with the Holy Spirit of power to accomplish God's purpose on Earth. Thus, this coming Messiah would reveal spiritual power through working miracles and wonders and he would prophesy truth from God.

The Messiah's Revealing in Type

Messiah is prophesied through the prophets and psalmists and shown in type throughout the Old Testament, especially through the Tabernacle. The fulfillment of these types is later seen in a remarkable way in the ministry of Jesus Christ.

Messiah is revealed to be the Son of God and the Lord of David speaking to the Lord God, showing His divinity and equality with God as His Son (Psalm 2:7–9; Psalm 110).

He is also shown to be a kinsman redeemer and a substitutionary sacrifice through the sacrificial system, often pictured as a lamb. And He is explicitly revealed as a sacrifice in Isaiah 53 who is *"wounded for our transgressions, ... bruised for our iniquities,"* and *"with his stripes we are healed."*

"... The LORD hath laid on him the iniquity of us all. ...

he is brought as a lamb to the slaughter, ... he bare the sin of many, and made intercession for the transgressors" (Isa. 53:5-6, 12). God knew that Messiah would die for the sins of the world and promised *"... thou shalt make his soul an offering for sin ..."* (Isa. 53:10).

This means that Messiah must be a sacrifice for the sin of the world and must be capable of being a sinless substitute to die in the sinner's place. Messiah would have to be sinless to die for the sins of others.

This Root and Stem of Jesse is declared to be the ruler of the government, the future Kingdom of God, and the government will sit upon His shoulder or under His authority (Isa. 9:6-7). He is Emmanuel, God with us, *"Wonderful, Counsellor, The mighty God, The everlasting Father, The Prince of Peace"* in Isaiah 9:6, meaning Messiah is equal with God.

The Messiah Is Prophesied To Be a Ruler Over Israel

In later days, Amos prophesied that God would *"raise up the tabernacle of David that is fallen"* (Amos 9:11). The Jews knew that this meant that God would unite the entire house of Israel, including Judah and Israel, into a future united kingdom. The fallen glory of the house of David would be reborn and they would live and serve under King Messiah.

Messiah was the one who is *"to be ruler in Israel; whose goings forth have been from of old, from everlasting"* (Micah 5:2), showing that Messiah is destined to be Israel's ruler and He had an eternal beginning. He is the Sun of Righteousness with healing in His wings, the Servant of God, His Chosen One, the one in whom God will put His Spirit, and He will judge the nations (Isa. 42:1).

The Coming of Messiah Is Foretold

Messiah was promised to be virgin-born (Gen. 3:15; Isa. 7:14) and to be born in Bethlehem (Micah 5:2). He had the role of providing salvation by His death (Isa. 53), to rule the Kingdom of God on Earth (Isa. 9:6), and to be a priest after the order of Melchizedek (Psalm 110:4).

There are about seventy astounding major prophecies of Messiah with three hundred thirty ramifications,[10] yet God promised to send the Messiah to fulfill all the promises, keep and fulfill the law, and bear the sins of man. He prophesied about the timing of the coming of Messiah in Daniel 9 and this prophecy would only be accomplished through the life of one man, Jesus Christ.

Jesus Came to Offer the Kingdom and His Messiahship to the Jewish People

At the appointed time, Jesus of Nazareth was virgin-born in Bethlehem from the tribe of Judah and the house of David. He lived a sinless life, fulfilling the law, giving forth the Word of God with power, showing His role as Messiah by His miracles, signs, and wonders, and offering the Kingdom to the Jews.

God Is with Us

Jesus not only claimed to come from God, but He also claimed to be the Son of God and at one with the Father or to be equal to God. He not only healed the multitudes, He also forgave sins, which no mere man could ever do.

Jesus was the only begotten Son of God, the unique essence of God wrapped in human flesh, and He was fully human and fully Divine, literally fulfilling the promise of a coming Emmanuel, "God with us" (Matt. 1:23). Jesus

---

10. Ray Konig, "Chart of Old Testament prophecies fulfilled by Jesus," Accessed on September 11, 2024, https://about.jesus.org

claimed to be Divine and proved it by His resurrection.

The Messiah Served the House of Israel

Jesus preached repentance and announced the coming of the Kingdom (Matt. 4:17), and foretold of His death on the cross and His resurrection (Matt. 16:21) as pictured in Psalm 22. He explained the spiritual nature of the coming Jewish kingdom and called for Israel to repent. Jesus also sent disciples to reach the Jewish people as they were sent specifically to the house of Israel.

Even his triumphal entry riding a donkey into Jerusalem, as prophesied in Zechariah 9:9, shows He fulfilled the role of the Messiah for Israel, and He originally restricted His ministry to Israel alone (Matt. 10:5–6; 15:24; Mark 7:27; John 1:11; Acts 10:36) to serve and redeem the house of Israel.

The Messiah Was Presented as the Savior

The Jews knew of a coming redeemer who would *"save his people from their sins"* (Psalm 22; Isa. 53, Matt. 1:21). Even his mother Mary realized that the birth of Messiah was the birth of her Savior (Luke 1:46–47). But primarily, the Jewish people were looking for a political king to save them from their oppression under the Romans rather than a redeemer.

Jesus was announced by the forerunner John the Baptist and was clearly revealed as the Redeemer when John said, *"Behold the Lamb of God, which taketh away the sin of the world"* (John 1:29). Thousands followed Him and many hundreds received His message and believed in Him.

Jesus showed that He was the Prophet, Priest, and King prophesied in the Old Testament. In John 14:6, He declared that He alone was the way, the truth, and the life; He was the only way to God, He spoke the Truth and was the Living

Word, and Jesus alone can give eternal life, pictured in living water and the bread of life and demonstrated in the power of the resurrection.

The Way to God

He preached the Gospel of the Kingdom, meaning that He preached that the Kingdom was near and the door to the Kingdom was spiritual. This was to be entered by being born again with a spiritual birth (John 3:3, 16).

His first sermon was teaching the spiritual life of the Kingdom — His Sermon on the Mount (Matt. 5–7). This sermon puzzled and confused the religious who were looking to earn a place in the Kingdom by their works.

Yet, Jesus demonstrated that the way to God was belief in God, not doing good works. The good works of believers were not the process of salvation but the fruit and evidence of their personal salvation. This sermon dealt with the heart of the individual and being prepared spiritually for the Kingdom.

The Abrahamic Covenant had offered salvation by believing in God, and the method of salvation and the way to God was still by grace through faith. The common people heard Him gladly, yet the religious leaders mostly rejected Jesus and His message. Instead, they were relying on their own works to provide them an outward appearance of righteousness while Jesus preached repentance and emphasized a new inner heart of righteousness.

Messiah's Rejection by Israel

This rejection by the religious leaders grew until eventually, they plotted to kill Him. Jesus knew of the betrayal under Judas Iscariot (Matt. 22:22) and that Judas' betrayal would result in Christ's death on the cross, but Jesus set His face, like a flint, to go to Jerusalem to die for the sins of mankind.

He had prophesied His death and resurrection three times and He knew the true purpose of His coming. Jesus said, *"... for I am not come to call the righteous, but sinners to repentance"* (Matt. 9:13) and *"The Son of man is come to seek and to save that which was lost"* (Luke 19:10).

Jesus knew that the Jews would reject the offer of the Kingdom and that He would turn His light to the Gentiles, preach in parables to the house of Israel, and He would be betrayed and die on the cross, bearing the sins of the world, and then rise again in power on the third day.

The Jewish leaders looked to accuse Jesus of breaking the Sabbath and tried in vain to find any sin or wrongdoing of Jesus. They then criticized Him in growing intensity until they accused Him of doing miracles in the power of the devil. As their hatred of Jesus grew, they then looked to capture and kill Him, eventually hiring Judas to betray Him.

After Jesus' triumphal entry into Jerusalem, Jesus was betrayed, unjustly tried, condemned, beaten, and cruelly crucified. Yet, God raised Him from the grave and He was seen alive by five hundred men before He ascended back to Heaven.

Jesus had been rejected by the Jewish people because He was not the Messiah they were expecting. They were looking for a king to rid them of oppression and for Messiah to establish His throne on Earth where the Jews could help rule with Messiah over others. But Jesus did not come the first time to establish a kingdom on Earth.

They did not realize the twofold purpose of Christ on Earth: He came first to provide salvation by His death and resurrection, and Jesus will come again to establish the Kingdom of God on Earth.

Jesus Fulfilled the Role of Messiah

Jesus did provide salvation to all who believe in Him alone

as their Savior in His first coming. In Jesus' second coming, He will judge the followers of the Antichrist and then establish a Millennial Kingdom of God ruling personally on Earth.

The Jews will then experience all the blessings of the Abrahamic, Davidic, Land, and New Covenants and they will live in the new Kingdom of Israel, serving God in His holy mountain and worshiping God in His holy Temple.

Jesus is the true Messiah of the Jews, fulfilling all the prophecies, and providing salvation. One day, He will come again and establish the eternal Kingdom of God. Jesus is the prophesied Prophet, Priest, and King, the Son of God in the flesh, and the only true Savior for whosoever would believe.

The Promise of Messiah

The seed of a woman (Gen. 3:15)
The Passover lamb sacrifice (Ex. 12:21-27)
The Son of God and Lord of David (Ps. 2, 110:1)
The kinsman-redeemer (Ruth 4:4-9; Lev. 25:47-55)
The sin bearer and offering for sin (Ps. 55)
Wonderful, Counsellor, Prince of Peace (Isa. 9:6)
The Mighty God, Everlasting Father (Isa. 9:6)
The prophet like Moses (Deut. 18:15-19)
Priest after Melchizedek (Ps. 110:4)
The scepter from Judah (Gen. 49), King of glory (Ps. 24)

The Messiah Prophecies Fulfilled

the Star from Jacob (Num. 24:17)
the line of David (2 Sam. 7:12-16)
Virgin Born (Isa. 7:14), In Bethlehem (Micah 5:2)
Would perform signs of healing (Isa. 35:5-6)
Would bring the New Covenant (Jer. 31:31)
Betrayed by 30 pieces of silver (Zech. 11:12-13)
Crucified (Ps. 22:16, Zech. 12:10)
the Resurrection (Job 19:25, Ps. 16:8-11)

CHAPTER THREE

THE WONDER OF THE JEWISH PEOPLE

The Wonderful Impact of the Jewish People

The Jewish people have produced many amazing inventions and discoveries in science throughout history such as the invention of stainless steel, the ballpoint pen, the television, the laser, the cell phone, the USB flash drive, and a host of others. They have contributed to the advancement of art and culture.

The list of Jewish musicians, famous and otherwise, in classical music of recent and current history is astounding. It would be very rare to find a classical orchestra anywhere worldwide without Jewish members. Many of the most famous performers of classical and pop music continue to be of Jewish descent.

Their impact in medicine such as creating many medical devices and cures for diseases, and their impact in all areas of education is widely known. Today in Israel, the Jewish people maintain a fully modern society with fine hospitals, medical clinics, and all the modern conveniences of a free society. They also impact the world culturally through their symphony orchestra and their many museums.

The world is blessed that the Jewish people have existed all over the world, and benefit from their impact on society in limitless ways. Yet, the Bible tells us that Israel would be a cup of trembling and a burdensome stone for the nations of the world. In other words, the nations would find Israel a problem for them in a variety of ways and be continually troubled by her existence.

No matter what good is done by the Jewish people

and by the nation of Israel, many people are opposed to the people and the nation. This resentment has caused the persecution of the Jewish people that has happened throughout history.

The History of Jewish Persecution

Israel was occupied by the Seleucid and Ptolemy Greeks, with especially harsh atrocities under the leader Antiochus Epiphanes about 190 BC.

They won their independence under Judas Maccabeus but soon were occupied by the Romans. The Jews led in two revolts of AD 68–70 (which resulted in the Roman destruction of the Jewish Temple) and AD 132–135 with a brief independence under Bar Kokhba, but then they were treated harshly by Emperor Hadrian and all Jews were forced to flee the land of Israel. Although Jews had settled in other lands previously, this began their total worldwide dispersion.

The Jews that returned later and remained in the land faced hardships with the Mameluke Arabs, the Crusaders, and later the Turks.

- In 1096, twelve thousand Jews were killed in Germany in three months.
- In 1290, the Jews were banished from England.
- In 1348, the Jews were blamed for the European plague and sorely persecuted.
- In 1492, under Ferdinand and Isabella, the Spanish Inquisition was launched. Thousands of Jews were killed and imprisoned, and one hundred and ten thousand were forced to flee for their lives. They were uprooted with no haven, protection, or home. (This same Inquisition also persecuted and killed thousands of Christians. Anyone non-Catholic was persecuted and killed.)

- In 1516, the first ghetto was created in Venice where Jews were herded and forced to live in poverty and squalor.

- In 1883, the largest Jewish population lived in Russia. The infamous pogroms were instituted and five hundred Jewish villages were ravaged by twelve hundred pogroms. Over sixty thousand people were killed, and many times that number were wounded, imprisoned, and persecuted. The Russians attacked, harassed, and robbed their Jewish neighbors and thousands fled their homes and country.

- Between 1933 and 1945, genocide of the entire Jewish nation was attempted by the Nazis. Under Hitler, these cruel and merciless Nazi German leaders killed at least six million Jews. Gas chambers, firing squads, and indescribable atrocities were perpetrated. In the same period, the fascists, the communists, and others persecuted the Jews, yet the nation miraculously survived.

- In the 1990s, the Arabs and Muslims tried to destroy the fledgling nation by attacking them five times (such as with SCUD missiles). Also, Israel was victimized by terroristic acts regularly.

- Since the year 2000, renewed violence in Israel has resulted in many deaths while peace talks are continually started and halted.

Jerusalem Is a Cup of Trembling

The Bible had prophesied that Jerusalem would be a cup of trembling throughout her history. In our current times, Jerusalem continues to be a cup of trembling. Earlier, Israel had drunk a cup of trembling and had her own problems (Isaiah 51:22–23).

Here, in Isaiah 51, God took from Israel the cup of trembling and gave it to her oppressors. Now, Israel has become the cup of trembling to other nations. Israel and Jerusalem seem to be a continual problem for other nations and both are constantly in the news.

Zechariah 12:1-3 says:

> *The burden of the word of the Lord for Israel, saith the Lord, which stretcheth forth the heavens, and layeth the foundation of the earth, and formeth the spirit of man within him. Behold, I will make Jerusalem a cup of trembling unto all the people round about, when they shall be in the siege both against Judah and against Jerusalem. And in that day will I make Jerusalem a burdensome stone for all people: all that burden themselves with it shall be cut in pieces, though all the people of the earth be gathered together against it.*

The metaphor "cup of trembling" was taken from an earlier Babylonian phrase. This is the concept that the nations will become intoxicated with Jerusalem. When they challenge Israel or attack her, they will stagger and stumble like a man who is drunk from drinking deeply from a strong cup of wine and is no longer in control of his faculties. These nations will then react as if drunk with wine when logic and reason have disappeared and they then respond in an unreasonable and strange way, full of rage and hatred.

Israel Is Become a Burdensome Stone

Israel will also become a burdensome stone, which is a picture of an ancient farmer who finds a large, conspicuous stone in a key place on his field. As he tries to remove it, he finds that it is a sharp stone that cuts and lacerates him. The more he works to remove the stone, the more he is constantly injured, while the stone remains unmovable, steadfast, and unharmed.

The presence of the Jews in Jerusalem is seen to have the same effect on the nations, that as they oppose her and try to remove her, they will cut and lacerate themselves (or do damage to themselves). And yet, Israel will continue as if unharmed and unmovable.

Though all nations have not yet turned against Israel, all nations who oppose Israel will be torn asunder. Yet, it seems absurd that Israel would be a problem or even a nation of interest to most people of the Earth. Jerusalem is not a key city of the Earth in many respects. It has no natural resources, no river, no harbor, it is not a key point of world commerce, it has no strategic importance, and no geopolitical relevance.

And yet, the problems of Israel seem to be magnified to all the people of the world, continually and especially in favor of their enemies and in favor of the Muslims. For several hundred years under the Arabs, Jerusalem fell into dormancy, ruin, and devastation, and the city was not of any interest to the Arabs until it was discovered to be significant to the Jews, and then it suddenly became vital to Islam.

The Jewish People Return to Their Land

Although Moses had prophesied that the people of Israel would possess the land of Israel and then experience the eventual dispersion of the Jews (often called the diaspora), he even foresaw their later end-time return to Israel (Deuteronomy 30:1-3). Isaiah 11:11-12 gives us even more insight:

> And it shall come to pass in that day, that the Lord shall set his hand again **the second time to recover the remnant of his people**, which shall be left, from Assyria,

and from Egypt, and from Pathros, and from Cush, and from Elam, and from Shinar, and from Hamath, and from the islands of the sea. And he shall set up an ensign for the nations, and shall assemble the outcasts of Israel, and gather together the dispersed of Judah from the four corners of the earth [emphasis added].

After the Babylonian captivity, God regathered his people and they returned to the land of Israel under King Darius. Now in the last days, God will regather his people again to return to the land God had given them by covenant promise, the land they had earlier conquered, dwelt in for hundreds of years, and where their Temple stood under kings Solomon, Zerubbabel, and Herod.

This return of the Jews in the last days will come in two stages. We are now experiencing their first return in unbelief, but they will also return the second time in belief after Armageddon.

The beginning of this prophesied return began in the nineteenth century under Zionism. When encouraged by Theodore Herzl, the Jews began to return to the land. On May 14, 1948, David Ben Gurion declared Israel to be an independent nation, and she was recognized eleven minutes later by President Truman of the United States.

Many people thought that after the horror of the Holocaust and the many pogroms and ghettos of Europe, the Jews had finally found a homeland and they could now live in peace. But Israel was immediately attacked and had to fight off multiple nations, primarily Arab, who wanted to wipe out her existence.

Now, after fighting five wars and enduring unending terrorist attacks, Israel is being unjustly pushed to follow the Oslo Accords. This is a clear demand to divide the nation and give away half of the land to appease the Arabs. But it cannot end in anything but another war in which Israel would be pushed to lose by leaving her with unbelievable disadvantages while giving all advantages to her enemies, the Muslims.

Chuck Missler clearly sees the only obvious result of this supposed peace with the Oslo Accords:

> As we have repeatedly pointed out, the peace process that began at Oslo virtually guarantees a war in the Middle East. The entire charade is based on a false premise: it assumes that the Muslim ambitions can be appeased by reducing the borders of Israel, even though the Muslim leadership has repeatedly and clearly maintained — before, during, and after the Oslo Accords — that they will not rest until the very existence of Israel has been eliminated.
>
> They are insisting on what Israel cannot yield [the extermination of the complete people and land of Israel]. The legacy of hate that they inculcate their children with continues without any pretense of abatement.[11]

The Palestinian Attack on the Jews

Israel has had to endure and fight the continual problems and unimaginable atrocities of the Palestinian Liberation Organization (PLO), who want to kill all of the Jews and take all of the land. The PLO launched constant attacks on Israel from Jordan from 1949 to 1970 when King Hussein expelled Yasser Arafat and his army, forcing them to flee to Lebanon. From there, they continued their terrorist attacks until the PLO was forced to flee to Libya in 1992.

There can be no negotiation and appeasement of the PLO when their intention is the total annihilation of the Jewish race. Israeli Prime Minister Benjamin Netanyahu has

---
11. Chuck Missler, "Prognosis for Jerusalem? A Cup of Trembling," Koinonia House, Accessed on January 16, 2023, https://khouse.org

described the situation well: "If the Arabs were to put down their weapons today, there would be no more violence. If the Jews were to put down their weapons today, there would be no more Israel."[12]

For an example of the situation Israel faced with the terrorist organization the PLO, Marv Rosenthal gives us an overview:

> What are the true facts about Arafat's PLO henchmen?
>
> In 1972, the PLO invaded Munich's Olympic Village and slaughtered eleven unarmed Israeli athletes. In 1973, an arm of the PLO murdered the U.S. ambassador to the Sudan along with his deputy.
>
> In 1974, the PLO seized an Israeli schoolhouse, held more than one hundred people captive and murdered twenty. In 1978, the PLO waylaid a Tel Aviv bus and massacred thirty-three citizens. The PLO has hijacked the airliners of at least eight world airlines.
>
> The PLO aided, trained and applauded every anti-American force on Earth from North Vietnam to Libya, Cuba, Nicaragua and El Salvador. In the 1970s, the PLO planned and executed more than 1,500 attacks across Israel's border.
>
> Driven out of Jordan in 1970 by King Hussein in what became known as "Black September" (note this fighting and dispersion was Arab against Arab), they were helped into Lebanon by Syria. There, they quickly acted as a catalyst to start a civil war between Christian and Muslim Lebanese.
>
> Once they arrived in Lebanon, the PLO operated a "state with a state" — confiscating hospitals and homes, forcing young people into the militias, closing schools, commandeering licenses and passports,

---

12. David Reagan, *9 Wars of the End Times* (McKinney, TX: Lamb & Lion Ministries, 2023), p. 18.

raping, murdering and terrorizing an entire nation — and the world, for pragmatic reasons, remained silent.

Israel reluctantly moved against PLO-occupied areas in Southern Lebanon to protect the lives of her citizens in Northern Israel from relentless attacks launched from PLO bases and strongholds in Southern Lebanon which the United Nations peacekeeping force was to have prevented.[13]

Then a peace plan was brokered by Israel's Yitzhak Rabin and PLO's Yasser Arafat with the help of U.S. President Bill Clinton to sign an accord for Palestinian self-rule. A two-part agreement (signed in 1993 and 1995), the Oslo Accords is seen as the first step to the recognition of the two states of Israel and the PLO by each other.

This is the international acknowledgment of the PLO as Israel's partner in permanent negotiations about any remaining issues revolving around the Israeli-Palestinian conflict. The PLO recognized the State of Israel. Israel recognized the PLO as "the representative of the Palestinian people," no more, no less.[14]

The Problems with a Two-Party State

However, this accord did not create a separate Palestinian state inside of Israel, as is often supposed or believed. Yitzhak Rabin said, "We do not accept the Palestinian goal of an independent Palestinian state between Israel and Jordan. We believe that there is a separate Palestinian

---

13. Marv Rosenthal (October/November 1982), "I will make Jerusalem a cup of trembling!" *Israel, my Glory* Accessed on January 16, 2023, https://israelmyglory.org.

14. Israel PLO Recognition: Exchange of Letters between PM Rabin and Chairman Arafat, Archived 4 May 2015 at the Wayback Machine, 9 September 1993.

entity short of a state."[15]

But since this agreement, there has been constant pressure from outside nations, including the United States, for a two-state policy as the answer to the Palestinians. The Palestinians also do not want a two-party state. They do not want to coexist with Israel. Rather, they want to wipe Israel off the map and completely eradicate the existence of the Jewish people.

For four hundred years, a large portion of the Middle East and Turkey had been under Ottoman Turkish rule. This was primarily a Muslim kingdom with Turks and various Arabs all under one united kingdom. The modern Middle Eastern countries did not exist until they were partitioned as an outcome of the Turkish backing of Germany in the First World War.

As a result, the area of Palestine was taken by the British, and the area of Syria by the French. The Arabs of the region thought of Palestine as a part of Syria (as an Arab Syria or a Southern Syria), and neither Arabs nor Jews wanted to partition Palestine. Neither side wanted to cooperate in a two-party state.

When the British partitioned Palestine and called one part Trans-Jordan (or later Jordan) and planned to give the other part to the Jews, the Arabs assumed that all of the land was still Arab and now a part of Jordan. They would not accept even the possibility of a Jewish State. The late King Hussein of Jordan (grandfather of Abdullah) said, "The truth is Jordan is Palestine and Palestine is Jordan."[16]

The Arabs threatened war if the partition plan was implemented or if Israel declared statehood. As stated by

---

15. Chris Hodges (5 May, 1994), "Mideast accord: the overview; Rabin and Arafat sign accord ending Israel's 27-year hold on Jericho and the Gaza Strip," *New York Times*, Accessed on January 16, 2023, https://newyorktimes.com.

16. Quoted in the newspaper Al–Nahar Al–Arabi (December 26, 1981) and cited by Benjamin Netanyahu in *A Place Among the Nations*, p. 147.

David Ben-Gurion at the time, "There is no solution. We want the country to be ours and they want the country to be theirs."[17]

After the Jews immigrated to Palestine, bought their land from the Arabs, and eventually declared Israeli statehood, they were attacked by the Arab nations on all sides. Following an intense war, Israel won the rest of the land and declared her borders.

And yet, the concept of accomplishing a sole Arab state in Palestine to occupy the entire area has continued to be the Arab goal, the Arabs have long refused to acknowledge the existence of the state of Israel, and coexistence between the two people groups remain very tenuous with distrust on both sides.

The Palestinian Myth

Regarding the Palestinians, during the nearly nineteen hundred years that the Jews were exiled from their land: there was never a Palestinian state in the land of Israel. Jerusalem was never the capital of an Arab state. There is no Palestinian identity or language. The Palestinian people have only been in the land for the last generation or two and are a mix of many nationalities, many of which are non-Arab. They were not forced to leave the land but left of their own free will.

In one revealing study of the Palestinians it states,

> There is no such a thing as a Palestinian people, a Palestinian culture, a Palestinian language, or a Palestinian history. There has never been any Palestinian state, neither any Palestinian archaeological finds nor coinage. The present-day Palestinians are an Arab people, with Arab culture, Arabic language and Arab history. They

---

17. Randall Price, *Fast Facts on the Middle East* (Eugene, OR: Harvest House Publishers, 2003), p. 30.

have their own Arab states from where they came into the Land of Israel about one century ago to contrast the Jewish immigration. That is the historical truth.[18]

The Roman emperor Hadrian renamed the Roman province of Judea to Syria Palaestina in the early second century AD to humiliate the Jewish people and to erase the Jewish history with the land.

Prime Minister Golda Meir said,

> There is no such thing as a Palestinian Arab nation. Palestine is a name the Romans gave to Israel with the express purpose of infuriating the Jews. Why should we use the spiteful name meant to humiliate us?[19]

According to *Israel Today News*,

> The Saudi Crown Prince recently said, "I don't care about the Palestinians." In a closed conversation with the American Secretary of State Anthony Blinken, the Saudi Crown Prince Mohammed Bin Salman said what we have been writing for years: the Arab governments don't care about the Palestinians at all.
>
> When did he say that? On the same day that Hezbollah leader Hassan Nasrallah was sent several floors lower than his underground bunker, to hell, by Israeli fighter jets in Beirut.
>
> Israel's latest strikes against the Iranian axis of evil in the Middle East are bringing new winds of change to the Middle East. This is encouraging the Sunni governments and giving the Saudi kingdom new hope for normalization with Israel, which had been put on

---

18. Myths, Hypotheses and Facts.
19. *Israeli Global News / Jerusalem Post*, 25 November 1995

the "back burner" in recent years.[20]

Thus, why should Israel give the land of Israel to a people who never possessed the land as a nation or identity? It is also interesting that all the surrounding Arab nations do not want to help the Palestinians but see them as a problem for Arabs as well as Jews.

King of Jordan, Abdullah II, gives insight. While speaking on AFP television in Berlin, Germany, in referring to the Palestinian conflict he said,

> The whole region is on the brink of falling into the abyss, that this new cycle of death and destruction is pushing us towards. The threat of this war expanding is real.
>
> On the issue of refugees coming to Jordan, and I think I can speak quite strongly on behalf, not only of Jordan as a nation, but of our friends in Egypt, that is a red line! Because I think that is the plan by certain of the usual suspects to try and create de facto issues on the ground.
>
> There will be no refugees in Jordan, no refugees in Egypt. This is a situation of humanitarian dimension that has to be dealt with inside of Gaza and the West Bank, and not to try and push the Palestinian challenge and their future on to other people's shoulders.[21]

Palestinian leaders have promoted a history that does not exist, have refused to live with the Jews in the land of Israel, and have no friends with any Arab countries. This hatred has led to more terrorism and fighting while Israel wants to live at peace in the land.

---

20. "New winds are blowing in the Middle East: Mohammed Bin Salman and the dwindling importance of the Palestinians," *Israel Today News:* 09/30/2024

21. King Abdullah II of Jordan, AFP television

The Increase of Terrorism in Israel

As a result, the PLO became the Palestinian Authority, ruling the area of Gaza and continuing its terrorist operations. The Palestinians have continued to operate terrorism inside of Israel, and have openly joined forces with Hamas, Palestinian Islamic Jihad, and other terrorist organizations, and even publicly recognized the involvement of terrorist groups in trying to pressure Israel to bow to their demands.

Hezbollah has taken the terrorist lead in Lebanon, primarily being funded and led through Iran. The country of Syria and other Arab nations, also constantly assisted by Iran, continued to move weapons through Syria to Lebanon to operate missile attacks and other forms of terror. And the many terrorist groups have continued to operate maneuvers of horror and terror to accomplish their goals.

As a matter of fact, it is widely thought that the attempt to get nuclear weapons by Iran is another part of their firsthand involvement in trying to help, influence, and even lead the terrorist attacks on Israel and that they are the primary movers behind a push for Israel's demise, as well as supporting terrorist involvement from many other Muslim nations.

Meanwhile, the United States has varied its view of how to be involved in helping Israel. While openly declaring her total commitment to Israel as our key national partner and friend in the Middle East, the United States has wavered in her commitment to Israel's declaration of independence.

This has partly been a variation in the conservative or liberal stand with which political party was in power at any given time in the United States. But, in recent years, it has come down to trying to appease the Arab nations to continue the export of Middle East oil to the world.

Marv Rosenthal again sees the current situation very clearly:

The American administration has clearly turned from total support of Israel to tactics that could one day cause her downfall.

Fundamentally, our government has decided that the better way to keep Russian influence out of the Middle East and the oil flowing is to court the friendship of so-called moderate Arab nations. To do this, Israel is being pressured to make concessions which jeopardizes her security.[22]

The partitioning of the land, the killing of the Jewish people, and the injustice of all human rights of the Jewish people all make the situation absolutely untenable. (As an example, the Muslim concepts of the Jews are so exceedingly antisemitic that it is believed by many extreme Muslim people that Jews are not even human).

The Claim to the Jewish Holy Land

Fundamentally, the Jews want their own homeland, the city of Jerusalem, and the Temple Mount to restart their system of worship again. They have won back all of these lands and more through fighting wars when they were attacked and yet won each war in amazing ways of God's providence.

The Jews now seek to pray on the Temple Mount as the first step to a form of worship, and one day they want to rebuild their Jewish Temple on their most holy site. The Temple Mount is their *most holy site* and the very foundation of their worship. This location has always historically been the center of their worship.

Meanwhile, the Arabs claim that the Temple Mount is

---

22. Marv Rosenthal (October/November 1982), "I will make Jerusalem a cup of trembling!" *Israel, my Glory* Accessed on January 16, 2023, https://israelmyglory.org

their *third most holy site*. They do not want to admit that the Jews ever existed as a people in Israel and ever had a Temple in Jerusalem, even though their earlier printed guidebooks to the Temple Mount clearly stated that this was the location of Solomon's Temple. They do not want to allow the Jews to even pray there and have repeatedly started riots to stop prayer!

After several riots and violence in 2022 at the Temple Mount over the issue of Jews praying there, now they are protesting again the Jewish *presence* on the Temple Mount. This pretense was claimed in 2000 when Prime Minister Ariel Sharon walked on the Temple Mount and it is being claimed again.

A recent visit to the Temple Mount by an Israeli minister is just one example of the concepts held by the Arabs and the world community and the continued problems for Israel. A review of this incident will give insight into the thinking of both the Jews and the Arabs.

A Visit to the Temple Mount by Israeli Minister Ben-Gvir

On January 3, 2023, Israeli National Security Minister Itamar Ben-Gvir made a thirteen-minute stroll on the Temple Mount, which resulted in an international uproar of complaints by many political groups. While he did not go near any Muslim religious sites, such as al-Aqsa or the Dome of the Rock, and he did not attempt to pray, Ben-Gvir made a short statement and left in peace. As reported in *The Jewish Press,*

> On the 10th day of Tevet, Itamar Ben-Gvir declared, "Our government will not surrender to the threats of Hamas. The Temple Mount is the most important place for the people of Israel, and we maintain the freedom

of movement for Muslims and Christians, but Jews will also go up to the mountain."[23]

Another source from *Fox News* continued with more of the short statement made by Ben-Gvir: "His visit, recorded by video, included a pointed moment in which he stared into the camera and said, 'We don't give in. We don't surrender. We don't blink' — a reference to the Jewish claim to the site."[24]

As a result of this peaceful stroll on the Temple Mount, the Arabs immediately tried to make this an international incident and various political groups responded. The Palestinian Authority claimed that Ben-Gvir's visit to the Temple Mount would lead to violence.

They tried to escalate the situation by telling the blatant lie saying that Ben-Gvir was storming the Temple Mount to attack the al-Aqsa mosque, and claiming that this would result in a change in the status quo (the Jews currently being unable to pray on the Temple Mount) and that it was a declaration of war. They even accused the Israelis of being "the occupational government" while they, as Muslim Arabs, were occupying or living in the land of Israel.

Israeli ambassador to the U.N., Gilad Erdan, quickly exposed the ludicrous and outlandish claims by the Arab leaders and terrorists accusing Ben-Gvir of attempting to change the status quo, of trying to start a war, or of doing anything illegal or out of the norm for anyone, including any Jew. "Minister Ben-Gvir's recent visit to the Temple Mount was not an incursion into al-Aqsa or any other fabrication that the Palestinians branded his visit as. Erdan also proclaimed that 'Jews are allowed to visit the Temple

---

23. David Israel, "Ben-Gvir Ascends to Temple Mount on Fast of Tevet Commemorating Siege of Jerusalem," *The Jewish Press*, Accessed on January 3, 2023. https://jewishpress.com

24. Peter Aiken, "Israeli Ambassador slams UN for meeting over visit to Temple Mount: The United Arab Emirates called for an urgent session to address Ben–Gvir's visit." *Fox News*, Accessed on January 14, 2023, https://foxnews.com

Mount. Every Jew!'"[25]

Quin Hillyer of the *Washington Examiner* has responded:

U.S. Senator Ted Cruz (R–TX) is right to blast Biden administration officials for siding with Palestinians against Israeli visits to the Temple Mount. He also is right to blast the administration for *repeatedly* siding against Israel, which essentially means siding with Islamic terrorists.

The Temple Mount is the holiest site in Judaism. Any restriction on Jewish use of the site should be anathema. Muslims or any others who insist otherwise have no moral standing.

Ben-Gvir was there for less than 15 minutes, and he did *not* pray, although he and his allies long *and quite reasonably* have said that Jews have every right to pray there, too. Less than six years ago, by the way, then National Security Minister Gilad Erdan visited the Temple Mount without major incident.

The Biden administration, though, is reflexively pro-Palestinian and openly hostile to Israeli Prime Minister Benjamin Netanyahu. Its representatives quickly worked themselves into a lather. Rather than tamping down tensions by calmly saying that a mere visit to the Temple Mount is nothing extraordinary, it adopted the Palestinian line that it was a massive provocation. In doing so, it ratifies, rather than deters, overreactions to what should be a total non-issue.

"The Biden administration's pathological obsession with undermining Israel is endangering the national security of America and our allies," Senator Ted Cruz said. "A visit by a minister from Israel's government to

---

25. Ibid.

a site inside Israel is not a challenge to any status quo arrangement, and it should not be controversial for a Jew to visit the holiest site in Judaism.

"The statements from the Biden White House and State Department, which suggest otherwise, will further destabilize the Middle East and risk inciting terrorism. They convince Palestinian officials that compromise is unnecessary because Democrat administrations will coerce our Israeli allies into making dangerous concessions."

Appropriately, Cruz provided context by listing numerous other ways the Biden administration has acted in ways remarkably anti-Zionist. For example, the administration "prohibited even mentioning the 'Abraham Accords,' sought to open a Palestinian consulate in Israel's capital Jerusalem, unleashed the FBI against the Israeli army, publicly ostracized parts of Israel's democratically elected government, [and has brought] officials from the terrorist Palestinian Liberation Organization to Washington D.C."

Cruz is correct in describing Biden's antipathy to traditionalist Israelis as "pathological." A truth-telling U.S. administration dedicated to fairness would insist that every human being has the right to peacefully visit the location and would try to persuade the Muslims that everybody, especially descendants of the Jews who worshiped there first, should be allowed to pray there, too.

Kowtowing to Islamic demands merely encourages Islamist violence. The Biden administration, not Netanyahu's, is the one acting unacceptably.[26]

---

26. Quin Hillyer, "Yes, Israeli officials have the right to visit the Temple Mount and pray there, too," *Washington Examiner*, Accessed on January 8, 2023, https://washingtonexaminer.com

The History of Modern Arab-Jewish Conflicts

The violence and deep hatred by Muslim terrorists have resulted in many violent conflicts. Dr. Randall Price lists thirty-three conflicts between the Arabs and the Jews since the time of Abraham, nineteen of which occurred since their return and the founding of the State of Israel. Dr. David Reagan sees the following eleven major Arab-Jewish conflicts since the founding of modern Israel:

- The War of Independence (1948-1949)
- The Suez War (1956)
- The Six-Day War (1967)
- The War of Attrition (1967-1970)
- The Yom Kippur War (1973)
- The First Lebanese War (1982)
- The First Intifada (1987-1993)
- The Second Intifada (2000-2005)
- The Second Lebanese War (2006)
- The First Gaza War (2008-2009)
- The Second Gaza War (2014) [27]

The October 7 Hamas Attack on Israel

On October 7, 2023, terrorist organization Hamas of Gaza committed an unprovoked attack on Israelis in a nearby town in southern Israel. They attacked the people, tortured and killed the children in front of the parents, brutally raped the women, and viciously killed and dismembered over twelve hundred unarmed, defenseless Jews. This resulted in an immediate Israeli-Gaza war, where Prime Minister Netanyahu vowed to wipe out the existence of Hamas.

Prime Minister Benjamin Netanyahu described the

---

27. David Reagan, *9 Wars of the End Times*, p. 18.

attack before the U.S. Congress. On July 24, 2024, he said,

> Like December 7, 1941, and September 11, 2001, October 7 is a day that will forever live in infamy. It was the Jewish holiday of Simchat Torah. It began as a perfect day. Not a cloud in the sky. Thousands of young Israelis were celebrating at an outdoor music festival. And suddenly, at 6:29 am, as children were still sleeping soundly in their beds in the towns and kibbutzim next to Gaza, suddenly Heaven turned into Hell. Three thousand Hamas terrorists stormed into Israel. They butchered 1,200 people from 41 countries, including 39 Americans.
>
> Proportionately, compared to our population size that's like 20 9/11s in one day. And these monsters raped women, they beheaded men, they killed parents in front of their children and children in front of their parents. They dragged 255 people, both living and dead, into the dark dungeons of Gaza.
>
> Israel has already brought home 135 of these hostages including seven freed in daring rescue operations.[28]

After the brutal attack, extremely difficult fighting ensued, with Hamas using the Palestinian people as pawns and human shields. Meanwhile, Israel was pressured to do nothing in retaliation or to stop the difficult fight with Hamas. The nation of Israel gave over 140 million dollars to the Palestinian Authority as a part of humanitarian aid for the Palestinian people,[29] which unfortunately will filter back as support for weapons for Hamas.

While America first supported Netanyahu and Israel's

---

28. Benjamin Netanyahu, "Netanyahu's 2024 Address to Congress," Haaretz, Accessed on August 22, 2024, https://haaretz.com

29. "Israel Okays New Payment of Over $140 Million to Palestinian Authority," NDTV World, Accessed on September 4, 2024, https://ndtv.com

war with Hamas, the liberal politicians tried to get a ceasefire to give time for more weapons for the terrorists and there were liberal pro-Palestinian demonstrations in America. It is now known that many of the anti-Israeli demonstrations in America were sponsored by Iran. However, most Americans are deeply committed to Israel and the preservation of the Jewish people.

While political situations will continue to transpire and perspectives change, there will continue to be many future situations of unrest, violence, terrorism, and fighting. Nations will be troubled and new stories of tensions, unrest, and killing will occur. Does the Bible tell us any solution to these problems? What is the prophetic future for these nations?

The Times of the Gentiles

When the Antichrist comes to power with a semblance and promise of final peace, which will later be revealed as false peace, the existence of Israel and control of Jerusalem will continue to be a "stone of stumbling" and a "cup of trembling" until the final battle of Armageddon and the victory of Jesus Christ over the Antichrist and his forces.

Jesus told us about the situation of unrest in Israel continuing during the times of the Gentiles in Luke 21:24: *"... Jerusalem shall be trodden down of the Gentiles, until the times of the Gentiles be fulfilled."*

The prophet Daniel gives us a prophetic timeline into the various kingdoms of the Gentile world until the end-time kingdom of Messiah, the Millennial Kingdom of Jesus.

The "times of the Gentiles" began with King Nebuchadnezzar of Babylon, and will continue until the coming world leader, known popularly as the "Antichrist," makes his appearance and is later dealt with at Armageddon. Nebuchadnezzar had a dream in which he saw a colossal man-image (Daniel 2). This dream was interpreted by Daniel to be an outline of future Gentile civilizations.

This span of Gentile political domination of Israel has lasted more than twenty-six hundred years. In the dream of Daniel 2, the *head of gold* (the first kingdom) symbolized the Babylonian Empire under the autocratic rule of Nebuchadnezzar. The *breast and arms of silver* (the second kingdom) represented the Medo-Persian Empire. The *belly and thighs of brass* (the third kingdom) symbolized the Grecian or Hellenistic Empire. And the *two legs of iron* (the fourth kingdom) represented the fourth empire.

This fourth empire was first seen as a United Roman Empire, then a Divided Roman Empire comprising the eastern division under Byzantine supremacy and the western division under the rule of the Caesars in Rome. This would later become a ten-division empire in the last days and finally, the Messianic Kingdom will overcome all the earlier empires to become the ultimate Kingdom of Christ.

It was predicted that Israel would be "trodden down by the Gentiles," thus, controlled by Gentile nations, during this period. Antichrist will rise out of one of the ten kingdoms of the last days, symbolized by the ten toes of the colossal man-image, and he is destined to be the last Gentile world ruler.

Historical Details of the Last Gentile Empire

Daniel 7 gives us a similar picture of these coming empires during the times of the Gentiles with a few variations and distinctions of additional information. In Daniel 7, we have the presentation of the Babylonian Empire in the lion with eagle's wings and the Medo-Persian Empire in the lopsided bear, showing the dominance of Persia, and it is seen eating three ribs demonstrating the conquering of Lydia, Babylonia, and Egypt.

The leopard with wings of a weak bird is less majestic and grand than the lion or bear but is also more swift and represents the conquests of Alexander the Great, whose swift-moving empire was divided into four kingdoms. These were *Ptolemy* over Egypt, Palestine, and Arabia Petrea; *Seleucus* over Syria, Babylonia, and as far east as India; *Cassander* over Macedonia and Greece; and *Lysimachus* over Thrace and Bithynia.

The fourth beast was nondescript; it was different and more ferocious than all the earlier beasts, and broke all earlier empires to pieces. This final beast had ten horns, signifying ten kings or kingdoms, and then the rising of another eleventh horn or ruler.

This last ruler, seen as the "little horn," uproots three of the ten horns or kings and kills them, and the other seven horns or kings respond by giving full allegiance and submission to the eleventh "little horn." This kingdom is different because it institutes a new kind of rule, namely imperialism.

While earlier kingdoms were absolute monarchies with autocratic and usually oppressive rule, these kingdoms normally appointed rulers of conquered lands from the local people. The Babylonians allowed Jewish rule through Zedekiah and Gedaliah; Medo-Persia used Zerubbabel and Nehemiah; and the Greeks allowed the Jewish high priests to rule.

But Rome sent Romans such as Pontius Pilate to rule, bringing the rule of imperialism from Rome. Imperialism has continued in several forms to this day, but not always from Rome. A future Roman Empire (or Revised Roman Empire) was never prophesied in the biblical text, but this style of rulership, the rule of imperialism, would continue in various forms from different centers.

There was first the "united stage" under Rome, then

the "two-division stage" of the Roman Empire from AD 364, when Emperor Valentinian divided the Empire into an East-West division. The centers of power have moved from Rome in the west and Byzantium/Constantinople/Istanbul in the east to other centers of power over time.

In the east, Russia rose as the third Roman Empire and the leaders called themselves czars, which is Russian for Caesar. In the West, power shifted to France in AD 800, where Charlemagne declared his kingdom the Holy Roman Empire; it later shifted again to Germany and the leaders called themselves kaisers, which is German for Caesar.

The Future Last Days Gentile Empire

The later days stage of this empire will be the ten-division empire which will become a full one-world government. Antichrist will rise from this ten-division empire and assume power. The Antichrist will "confirm a covenant of peace" with Israel leading to a period of false peace and security until he begins the first world war of the Tribulation period, resulting in millions of deaths from war, famine, pestilence, and even animal attacks. A new one-world religion will also kill millions of believers during this period.

Later, the Antichrist will kill three of the ten kings, and the other kings will submit to his authority. He will then demand worship as a god and will unleash his wrath against the Jewish people and they will flee for their lives. He will continue to persecute and kill the Jews until he makes one last unsuccessful attempt to exterminate the Jews.

At the battle of Armageddon, Antichrist will attempt to kill all of the Jewish people and wipe out the entire Jewish nation. They will turn to the Lord Jesus in repentance and belief as an entire nation. However, Antichrist will be overcome by Christ at His revelation and he and the False Prophet will be sent to the flames of Hell, which will conclude "the times of the Gentiles."

After the seven-year rule of Antichrist in the Tribulation period, Jesus will return in victory at His glorious appearance and subdue the Antichrist and his forces at the Battle of Armageddon. Then He will set up God's final Kingdom of peace on Earth.

Antichrist and his forces will be defeated and destroyed by the coming of Christ Jesus who will overcome them and the Jewish remnant will be saved. Then Jesus will descend to Earth and establish His Millennial Kingdom, where He will rule for a thousand years as King of Kings and Lord of Lords.

Where Are We in This Timeline?

Will there be peace in Jerusalem? Apparently, only when the Prince of Peace comes to Jerusalem and takes over the world as the true bringer of peace. When He comes, the song of the angels will be fulfilled, *"Glory to God in the highest, and on earth peace, good will toward men"* (Luke 2:14).

Until those later momentous end-time days, and currently, while the Arab nations and various opponents of Israel are kept at bay, Jews will continue to fight for peace and the existence of their nation, ownership of their land, and the right to worship in their city.

This worship aspect is continued in a strong religious move by the more orthodox Jews, who believe in the Bible literally and want to follow God as their Jewish faith teaches. By actually trying to believe and practice their faith, they are seen as religious extremists, and yet they are only going back to their historic roots and faith.

In current times, the Temple Institute and other milder

groups are encouraging the rebuilding of the Jewish Temple, the search for the Ark of the Covenant, and the ashes of the red heifer. They are also raising new red heifers to procure a possible candidate for a renewed sacrifice.

These Levitical Jews are trained priests, part of the Cohanim (the priestly line of Jews from the Levitical line of Cohan) and they are daily living by the Jewish law. These religious Jews want to peacefully restart each area of their Jewish worship, which would require a rebuilt Temple and renewed sacrifices and they are working to accomplish these goals.

As of today, the Jews have returned to the land and they are fulfilling the promises of a people who will return in unbelief, endure persecution, and later turn to God and possess all the future promises of a Millennial Kingdom for Israel. The Bible promises that they will always continue to occupy the land of Israel no matter the opposition, difficulties, fighting, or even future wars. Although Israel has difficult days ahead in coming wars and persecution, Israel will be helped by God to endure as a nation and people for all her future.

The Times of the Gentiles (Dan. 2)

the head of gold - the Babylonian Empire
the breast and arms of silver - the Medo-Persian Empire
the belly and thighs of brass - the Grecian Empire
the two legs of iron - the united Roman Empire
a divided Roman Empire: (eastern) Byzantium, (western) Rome
a last days ten-division empire

Historical Details of the Gentile Empires (Dan. 7)

the Babylonian Empire - the lion with eagle's wings
the Medo-Persian Empire - the lopsided bear
the Greek Empire - the leopard with 4 wings
the Roman Empire - the fourth beast has ten kingdoms
In the East, Russia and czars, the third Roman Empire
In the West, Germany and kaisers, the Holy Roman Empire

The Last Days Gentile Empire (Rev. 13, 17-19)

the ten-division empire becomes the one-world government
the rise of the eleventh horn - Antichrist
the one-world religion and peace covenant with Israel
the seven-year Tribulation period
three kings are killed - seven kings submit
the battle of Armageddon - Antichrist is defeated
the Millennial Kingdom

CHAPTER FOUR

THE POSSIBLE ISRAEL WAR OF PSALM 83

When students of the Bible research the future of Israel, it is very clear from the Bible that Israel will have several future conflicts and wars until the Second Coming of Jesus, when after Armageddon, He sets up His Millennial Kingdom on Earth. Because the future wars are described in numerous places, and various details are added by multiple Old Testament prophets, it seems to be unclear to many Bible researchers just how many wars for Israel are still future.

Future wars and terrorist attacks seem to be a foregone conclusion for Israel. Repeatedly, her enemies announce Israel's doom. Jack Kelly of Rapture Ready reminds us,

> Hezbollah says that Israel's disappearance after the next war is an established fact. Iran's president has called Israel a dirty microbe and a savage animal that will soon disappear in a flash. The commander in chief of Iran's army predicts that millions will soon receive the joyous news of Israel's destruction. Israel's chief of staff warns of a "tough ordeal" coming soon.[30]

Thus, by the multiple threats of war and continued violence and terrorism, what is the future situation for a war of Israel mentioned in the Bible?

Perhaps the most in-depth studies and published work on this subject is by Bill Salus, who believes that there are as many as fourteen future wars and conflicts for Israel as

---

30. Jack Kelley, "Psalm 83—Preview of a Coming Attraction," Accessed on September 4, 2024, https://raptureready.com

he describes in great detail in his in-depth books. In some respects, the views of Joel Rosenberg are similar to Bill Salus. While other authors also describe their view of these future wars, another prominent viewpoint is presented by Dr. David R. Reagan, who believes there are eight or nine future wars for Israel, as described in his interesting book *Nine Wars of the End Times*.

Each of these Bible prophecy authors has presented solid research in this area and shows that there are many conflicts and fighting of nations with Israel. However, this book's author takes the biblical viewpoint that there are four future wars for Israel and that all of the biblical references were either earlier fulfilled or that they will be folded into and occur together with these future four conflicts.

These four future wars for Israel will be the Russian invasion of Israel joined with a confederation of other nations (Ezek. 38–39), the World War I of the Tribulation beginning with the second Seal Judgment of Revelation 6:3–4, the middle Tribulation war (World War II of the Tribulation) in Daniel 11, and the Campaign of Armageddon in Revelation 19 (World War III of the Tribulation).

The Prophecy of Psalm 83

Sometimes, when future wars are mentioned, the first possibility given is the mention of Israel being surrounded by her enemies on her national borders in Psalm 83. This Psalm has been controversial because even premillennial and pretribulational scholars hold different viewpoints of the psalm.

Note, first, the wording of Psalm 83:

> *Keep not thou silence, O God: hold not thy peace, and be not still, O God. For, lo, thine enemies make a tumult: and they that hate thee have lifted up the head. They have*

taken crafty counsel against thy people, and consulted against thy hidden ones. They have said, Come, and let us cut them off from being a nation; that the name of Israel may be no more in remembrance. For they have consulted together with one consent: they are confederate against thee: The tabernacles of Edom, and the Ishmaelites; of Moab, and the Hagarenes; Gebal, and Ammon, and Amalek; the Philistines with the inhabitants of Tyre; Assur also is joined with them: they have holpen the children of Lot. Selah. Do unto them as unto the Midianites; as to Sisera, as to Jabin, at the brook of Kison: Which perished at Endor: they became as dung for the earth. Make their nobles like Oreb, and like Zeeb: yea, all their princes as Zebah, and as Zalmunna: Who said, Let us take to ourselves the houses of God in possession. O my God, make them like a wheel; as the stubble before the wind. As the fire burneth a wood, and as the flame setteth the mountains on fire; So persecute them with thy tempest, and make them afraid with thy storm. Fill their faces with shame; that they may seek thy name, O LORD. Let them be confounded and troubled for ever; yea, let them be put to shame, and perish: That men may know that thou, whose name alone is JEHOVAH, art the most high over all the earth.

Psalm 83 is a poignant example of the continual hatred of the Arab people and other Islamic nations for the Jews and the nation of Israel. This hatred was begun through the descendants of Ishmael and Esau and was first mentioned in Numbers 20:14–21. This hatred and enmity have continued throughout biblical history into modern history.

In Psalm 83, the psalmist wants God to note a united conspiracy against Israel (vs. 1–3). These people want to so completely destroy Israel that even the name of Israel will no longer be remembered (vs. 4).

This concept of utter hatred and a desire for complete annihilation of the nation of Israel has continued into the times of modern history, especially by the Islamic nations of the Middle East. These nations are primarily Arab and hold strong hatred for Israel.

As an example, just before the Six-Day War, when announcing his upcoming invasion and war with Israel in 1967, Egyptian president Gamal Abdul Nassar Hussein, commonly known as President Nasser, said, "The battle will be a general one and our basic objective will be to destroy Israel."[31]

Next in Psalm 83, the enemy nations consult together and make a confederation to attack and to totally destroy Israel (vs. 5). These enemy nations are listed in verses 6–8 and they are notated in detail later in this chapter.

The psalmist calls upon God to defeat these enemy nations as He led earlier in the defeat of the Midianites and others in various past conflicts (vs. 9–11). He asks that the Jews take possession of the houses of God (vs. 12).

And he asks that God overcome their enemies, rolling them like a wheel in the wind, (vs. 13), like a fire that starts with a small piece of wood and burns up an entire mountain range, (vs. 14), and that their enemies would be persecuted with a great storm like a hurricane or tornado to learn to fear the true and only God (vs. 15). As a result, in shame these defeated foes would seek the name of God, be confounded, their armies will perish, and finally they will turn to know and follow Jehovah as the true God of all the Earth (vs. 16–18).

Several things must be noted about this psalm. The psalm was written by Asaph during the life of David, or more

---

31. The Six-Day War: Statement by President Nassar to Arab Trade Unionists (May 26, 1967), Accessed on April 17, 2024, https://jewishvirtuallibrary.org

likely, by the sons of Asaph during the time of Jehoshaphat during the events of 2 Chronicles 20:1–25. It is considered to have been written by a Levite named Jahaziel, one of the sons of Asaph, in the days of Jehoshaphat (2 Chron. 20:14). It was probably written during this time of Israel's distress.[32]

Psalmists were also sometimes prophets in the Old Testament and Asaph was identified as a "seer" or prophet in 2 Chronicles 29:30 and he "prophesied according to the order of the king" or at the command of King David (1 Chron. 25:2). Jahaziel was also a prophet from the line of Asaph. Thus, one of these prophets gave us this psalm.

It is interesting to note that occasionally their prophecy was given in the form of a song, or a psalm. They may have sung the prophecy to the king instead of telling it to him. Mary and Zechariah both gave prophecy through song upon hearing about the birth of Jesus (Luke 1:46–56, 57–80).

At this time of Israel's history during the kingdom of Jehoshaphat, she was surrounded by the people of Ammon, Moab, and Mount Seir (the Edomites) and Jehoshaphat did not know a way that Israel could be saved (2 Chronicles 20:1–25). Jahaziel came and prophesied that they trust in God and the Levite priests were gathered to sing praise to God.

As the people praised God in music, the enemy armies attacked and killed each other until not one enemy was left alive. God had supernaturally delivered His people again. Dr. Reagan calls this *Israel's War of Worship* because God supernaturally delivered His people while they worshiped and praised the only true God, the Lord Jehovah, the Lord God Almighty.

But Psalm 83 mentions additional nations that were not

---

32. Ed Hindson, Gen. Ed., Woodrow Michael Kroll, "Psalms." *The Liberty Bible Commentary — Old Testament* (Nashville, TN: Thomas Nelson, 1982), p. 1087.

involved in the conflict with Jehoshaphat. Thus, the psalm must imply a future time of Israel being surrounded and saved from her enemies. Also, one of the primary purposes in the defeat of Israel's enemies is that they might know the name of the Lord.

There can be no greater delight than to see that the oppressors and enemies of Israel never again seek to destroy Israel and that they turn to God and seek His name (Ps. 83:16). Although the Arab and Islamic nations have never turned to the name of Jehovah and followed the true God of the Bible, they will turn to God after Armageddon at the Millennium and believe on the Lord.

The Nations of Psalm 83

The confederacy of nations mentioned in Psalm 83 are more than just the nations of Moab, Ammon, and Mount Seir (Edom), mentioned in the events of 2 Chronicles 20. These ancient nations of Psalm 83:6–8 match modern nations as identified by Dr. David Reagan,[33] except the Hagrites who were Arabs from the area of Syria.[34]

It is evident that these nations surround Israel and will threaten her very existence as a nation. Psalm 83:4 tells us these nations proclaim, *"Come, and let us cut them off from being a nation; that the nation of Israel may be no more in remembrance."*

So, the desire of this confederacy of Arab nations in Psalm 83 is to completely remove the existence of Israel from the Earth. Since the founding of the modern nation of Israel in 1948, there has been a unified desire by Arab nations and all Muslim countries to destroy the entire nation of Israel.

---

33. David R. Reagan, *9 Wars of the End Times*, p. 28.

34. Jack Kelley, "Psalm 83—Preview of a Coming Attraction," Accessed on September 4, 2024, https://raptureready.com

The Nations of Psalm 83

Edom	Palestinians and South Jordan
Ishmaelites	Saudi Arabia (Ishmael was the father of the Arab people)
Moab	Palestinians and Central Jordan
Hagrites (Hagarenes)	Syria
Gebal	North Lebanon
Ammon	Palestinians and North Jordan
Amalek	Arabs of the Sinai area
Philistia	Arabs of the Gaza Strip
Tyre	South Lebanon
Assyria	Syria and Iraq

Is Psalm 83 a Prayer?

One objection to this prophetic view of the psalm is the question: Is Psalm 83 a prayer? Some Bible scholars believe that Psalm 83 is an imprecatory prayer and not a Bible prophecy. For instance, popular Christian author Dr. Mark Hitchcock has said,

> It may be that constructing a separate end-time war out of Psalm 83 is reading too much into a text that is simply saying that Israel has been and always will be surrounded by enemies and that someday the Lord will finally deal with them.

Dr. Thomas Ice, executive director of the Pre-Trib Research Center explains,

> While I consider Bill Salus and others who take this view to be friends and fellow protagonists with the field of Bible prophecy; however, there comes a time when friends must speak out against a friend when what they teach is not really found in the Bible. That is why I am sounding the alarm concerning the so-called "Psalm 83 war."
>
> It is clear to me that Psalm 83 is an imprecatory request on behalf of the nation of Israel by Asaph 3,000 years ago. This is the reason that Psalm 83 is classified as a national lament. There is no prophecy in the Psalm.[35]

Dr. Andy Woods also remarks, "Psalm 83 does not contain the language of predictive prophecy. It's just a prayer of an imprecatory nature."[36]

Bill Salus responds to this objection by pointing out that many of the imprecatory psalms are of David dealing with personal enemies, while Psalm 83 is danger from enemies for the entire nation of Israel.

Three Views of Psalm 83 as Future Fulfillment

If a Bible commentator believes in a future prophetic fulfillment of Psalm 83, he usually comes to one of three possibilities. The recent wide-reaching review of Psalm 83 has been greatly enhanced through the books and study of Bill Salus. And this has resulted in various interpretations.

This author appreciates the study of many of these prophecy writers and understands that we agree on the

---

35. Thomas Ice, "Consistent Biblical Futurism," Accessed on July 24, 2024, https://www.pre=trib.org/pdfs/Ice-ConsistantBiblicalFuturism_13.pdf.

36. Andy Woods, *The Middle East Meltdown* #30 Video 9/11/21.

major points of future prophecy, such as the imminent Rapture of believers, the seven-year Tribulation, the Campaign of Armageddon, and the Millennial Kingdom of Christ. And we can still discuss, study, and hold variations of views in smaller points of study, such as these possible additional wars. Each of these various prophetic writers mentioned in this study believes in salvation by grace through faith, the inerrant, preserved Word of God, and a consistent literal interpretation of the Bible. Thus, this study is not an attack on anyone, but a refining of the views of this author with the Bible as to the identification of the future wars with Israel.

Dr. David Reagan has remarked that Bill Salus is a true "eschatologist" because "he brings an inquisitive attitude to God's Prophetic Word, and this attitude propels him to constantly search for end-time prophecies that may have been overlooked."

While this author strongly endorses renewed study and in-depth review of Bible prophecies, it is also important to correctly interpret Bible prophecy with a literal interpretation in its historical/grammatical setting. Also, caution must be taken to not use "newspaper *exegesis*," trying to find prophecy in every daily event, or to use *eisegesis*, trying to read into a text prophecy and interpretation that are not there. So, care must be taken and solid Bible study to come to a balanced and thorough understanding of the Bible.

Dr. Reagan believes that Psalm 83 has "clear end-time indicators. For instance, there is a reference to the fact that the outcome of this war will be a contributing factor in motivating nations to seek the name of Yahweh (verse 10) because they will realize that He is 'the Most High over all the Earth.'"

Dr. Reagan continues,

> What he [Salus] has argued was that Psalm 83 is a

prophecy about an end-time war that is yet to occur — a war between Israel and all the Arab states with whom it shares a common border. Psalm 83 had been considered to be simply a lament over the desire of the nations of the world to destroy Israel.

As a result of his own in-depth review of this psalm, Dr. Reagan concludes,

> There is no biblical fulfillment of Psalm 83. The Six-Day War could be a fulfillment in whole or in part — most likely a partial fulfillment in type. The complete fulfillment of Psalm 83 is most likely in the future, serving as the event that will bring a brief time of peace to Israel — as well as expanded territory and increased wealth. The future war will most likely pave the way for the War of Gog and Magog, probably because the outcome will prompt the Arab nations to call for Russia to come to their aid.[37]

Thus, in *the first view*, Dr. Reagan believes that there will likely be a war between the nations surrounding Israel before the Gog and Magog war of Ezekiel 38–39. He believes this could happen before or after the Rapture of believers, but Dr. Reagan thinks it will precede and prepare the way for the Russian Invasion of Israel.

Meanwhile, Bill Salus believes that this Psalm 83 war is one of the first of a series of wars and conflicts that will happen before the Rapture as well as before the Russian invasion of Israel. Salus believes this early war sets the stage for other future events.

Dr. Reagan summarizes Bill Salus's view:

> By placing Psalm 83 into the end-time puzzle as the first

---

37. David R. Reagan, 9 Wars of the End Times, p, 37.

of the wars, Salus contended that all the future events come into their appropriate alignment. His conclusion was that Israel's victory in the war will provide the nation with the peaceful atmosphere that Ezekiel 38 & 39 says will be existing when the War of Gog and Magog begins (Ezek. 38:8, 11, 19). It will also provide Israel with the territory and wealth that will provoke the Arab nations to call upon Russia and its allies to come to their rescue.

He further argued that by considering Psalm 83 to be an end-time war occurring before the War of Gog and Magog, it solves a major mystery. The mystery relates to the fact that the list of allied nations of Gog and Magog that are named in Ezekiel 38 does not list a single nation that has a common border with Israel. Instead, all the nations listed consist of an outer circle around Israel.[38]

Thus, in *the second view*, Bill Salus believes an even broader prospect of future wars and conflicts for Israel. He believes that the Psalm 83 war is only one of the first in a series of additional wars for Israel that occur before the Rapture. He would include the prophecy of Elam as an additional conflict with Iran, the passage of Isaiah 17 as the destruction of Damascus, Syria, and other conflicts.

While this author does not hold to his position, Bill Salus has done some fine research and his views deserve further investigation. Also, it has prompted renewed research into little-known areas of Bible study.

A third view of Psalm 83 is that it is a lament that also includes prophetic material but it has a different fulfillment. In this view, the Psalm was pictured typically in one of Israel's modern wars, such as the War of Independence of

---

38. Ibid., p. 27.

1948–1949, the Six-Day War of 1967, or the Yom Kippur War (רוּפֶּכ םוֹי) of 1973.

The most likely foreshadowing of this psalm was when Israel was surrounded and attacked by multiple Arab nations during the Six-Day War of 1967 and this is the position of most researchers looking for a more current fulfillment. Israel was attacked by Egypt and multiple other nations, and yet she was able to not only defeat all other nations, she also was able to expand her borders through a huge amount of territory she conquered. While later Israel returned the Sinai Peninsula to Egypt, she owned all the land she conquered.

Thus, Israel owns the land of Israel and all other disputed territory; Israel is not an occupying nation. She does not occupy any land of another nation, including the West Bank, the Golan Heights, or the Gaza Strip, but she rightfully won these lands in military conflict, as most other countries of the world won their lands. It is for racism and antisemitism that other nations do not recognize or trade with Israel and it is a fulfillment of the prophecy of Jerusalem being a cup of trembling and a burdensome stone (Zechariah 12:2–3).

The foreshadowing of a prophetic event in type is seen in several biblical events. When Isaiah was told of the coming birth of a baby in Isaiah 7:14, this was a prophecy of the coming of a virgin-born babe, the Messiah, coming to be the Savior and Redeemer of mankind.

While Isaiah's wife did bear a son, this was only an illustration or a type of the future final fulfillment in the virgin birth of Christ. This is not a partial or dual fulfillment of a prophecy, but rather a picture in type or illustration of the prophecy that has the only full, entire, and complete fulfillment at a future time.

In this third view, in Psalm 83 Israel is seen as being surrounded by her enemies in the Six-Day War. She overcame them with the supernatural help of God, and yet this was only a foreshadowing or illustration of a later and future complete fulfillment, as a type or picture of the final fulfillment. The entire fulfillment will be when the Arab nations and all other Gentile nations who oppose Israel surround her and threaten to destroy her very existence. They will be overcome by Jesus Christ in the Battle of Armageddon (Rev. 19) and then many Arab people left alive will turn to the Lord and believe on His name. Thus, the fulfillment of Psalm 83 will be at the Campaign of Armageddon.

The Arab nations have not been completely overcome in the past. Although they have been defeated in past wars, they will still operate as nations during the Tribulation period and will be finally overcome and united into Christ's Kingdom as a result of the Battle of Armageddon.

There has also never been a time in history when all people have turned to believe in the Lord. Yet, these verses teach that as a result of this conflict, *"men may know that thou, whose name alone is JEHOVAH, art the most high over all the earth."*

God will show His sovereignty over nations as He defeats the enemies of Israel and saves Israel as His chosen people, and He also uses this conflict to show His power and to demonstrate that He alone is God. The enemy nations will realize that there is only one true God and they will forsake all other false gods and turn to Jehovah as the only true God of the universe.

At this time, there will be believers in Christ from every people, tribe, tongue, and nation worldwide. And this group of believing people will also include people from all nations and tribes of the Middle East.

Prophecies Against Gentile Nations in the Major and Minor Prophets

While there are many prophecies about Israel throughout Scripture including her return and restoration in the Messianic Kingdom, it is interesting to note prophecies about the Gentile nations, which usually refer to coming judgment from God because of their mistreatment of Israel. This is especially true in the Major and Minor Prophets of the Old Testament.

While Israel was away from God, the Lord would send prophets to tell them to repent and turn to the Lord for blessing. In the same area of Scripture, God would also tell how He would judge the enemies of Israel.

In these passages, there is a remarkable contrast between the return and restoration of Israel and the details of a future Millennial Kingdom with a negative future for the Gentile nations. Clearly, for the Gentile nations, the Bible gives the details of their future judgment.

Isaiah — A. *The Condemnation of the Nations (Isa. 13–23)*
        The Fall of Babylon, Isa. 13:1–14:23
        Judgment on Assyria, Isa. 14:24–27
        Judgment on Philistia, Isa. 14:28–32
        Judgment on Moab, Isa. 15–16
        Judgment on Ethiopia, Isa. 18
        Judgment on Egypt, Isa. 19–20
        Judgment on Babylon, Isa. 21:1–10
        Judgment on Edom, Isa. 21:11–12
        Judgment on Arabia, Isa. 21:13–17
        Judgment on Jerusalem, Isa. 22
        Judgment on Tyre, Isa. 23
    B. *The Condemnation of the World (Isa. 24–35)*
        The Tribulation and Kingdom: The Little Apocalypse, Isa. 24–27
        The Six Woes, Isa. 28–33

The Coming Assyrian Invasion, Isa. 33
The Tribulation and Kingdom, Isa. 34-35
God's Wrath Against All the Nations, Isa. 34

Jeremiah — *The Prophecies Concerning the Gentile Nations (Jer. 45-51)*
Prophecies Against Egypt, Jer. 46
Prophecies Against Philistia, Jer. 47
Prophecies Against Moab, Jer. 48
Prophecies Against Ammon, Jer. 49:1-6
Prophecies Against Edom, Jer. 49:7-22
Prophecies Against Damascus, Jer. 49:23-27
Prophecies Against Arabia (Kedar and Hazor), Jer. 49:28-33
Prophecies Against Elam, Jer. 49:34-39
Prophecies Against Babylon, Jer. 50-51

Ezekiel — *The Prophecies Against Foreign Nations, Ezek. 25-32*
Edom's Future Destruction, Ezek. 35
The Removal of Israel's Foes, Ezek. 36:1-7
Israel's Rescue from Gog and Magog, Ezek. 38-39

Daniel — *The Times of the Gentiles and the Future Nations, Dan. 2*
The Four Beasts, Dan. 7:1-8
The Fourth Kingdom, Dan. 7:19-28
The Ram, Goat, and Small Horn, Dan. 8:1-27
Prophecies Concerning the Nations, Dan. 11:2-45

Joel — *The Invasion of Israel on the Day of the Lord, Joel 2:1-11*
The Judgment on the Day of the Lord, Joel 3:1-7

Obadiah — *The Destruction of Edom and the Day of the Lord, Obadiah 1:1–16*

Jonah — *The Warning to Nineveh, Jonah 2:1–9*

Nahum — *The Fall of Nineveh, Nahum 1–3*

Zephaniah — *Day of the Lord with the Gentile Nations, Zeph. 2:4–15 (Philistia, Moab and Ammon, Ethiopia and Assyria)*

Zechariah — *The Campaign of Armageddon, Zech. 14:1–5*
The Destruction of Israel's Enemies, Zech. 14:12–15

Malachi — *Edom's Continual Future Judgment, Malachi 1:4–5*
The Day of the Lord, Malachi 4:1–4

As a result of these prophecies, God has a plan for a renewed Israel with the Lord Jesus Christ as the King of Kings ruling in a Millennial Kingdom. God also judges the Gentile nations and afterward, many Gentiles are saved and join in the Millennial Kingdom of Christ.

Yet, in these same passages, we see the results of judgment on the Gentile nations from their wars with Israel, as well as other wrath and judgment of God. That is why this study will mention several conflicts of nations with Israel mentioned in this area of the Bible.

CHAPTER FIVE

THE POSSIBLE ISRAELI WAR WITH IRAN

Bible commentators who look for additional wars of Israel happening before the Tribulation and/or before the Rapture also look at other possible scenarios. Because of the current tensions with Iran, this nation is especially in the news with its continual unrest with Israel. Today, with the involvement of Russia and Iran, their support of terrorism in multiple countries, and the barrage of Israel with scores of missiles, there is a constant threat of war, especially from Iran.

Israeli Prime Minister Netanyahu described the Iranian danger to the U.S. Congress in 2024. He said:

> In the Middle East, Iran is virtually behind all the terrorism, all the turmoil, all the chaos, all the killing. And that should come as no surprise. When he founded the Islamic Republic, Ayatollah Khomeini pledged, "We will export our revolution to the entire world."
>
> Now, ask yourself, which country ultimately stands in the way of Iran's maniacal plans to impose radical Islam on the world? And the answer is clear: It's America, the guardian of Western civilization and the world's greatest power. That's why Iran sees America as its greatest enemy.
>
> Last month, I heard a revealing comment from the foreign minister of Iran's proxy, Hezbollah, and he said this, "This is not a war with Israel. Israel," he said, "is merely a tool. The main war, the real war, is with America."

But Iran understands that to truly challenge America, it must first conquer the Middle East. And for this, it uses its many proxies, including the Houthis, Hezbollah, and Hamas. Yet in the heart of the Middle East, standing in Iran's way is one proud pro-American democracy — my country, the State of Israel.[39]

In the current situation in the Middle East, there well may be a war between Iran with Israel. And because of the radical Islam goal of Iran, America could easily be pulled into the war to fight Iran also. Because of this, one of the most obvious questions is: Are there any Bible prophecies that include this nation? Is there a future war for Iran mentioned in the Bible? One Bible prophecy that points to Iran is the prophecy of Elam.

The Prophecy of Elam

Another interesting prophecy that has come under more intense scrutiny of late is the prophecy of Elam in Jeremiah 49:34–39. This is also a prophecy where various excellent Bible scholars hold different interpretations.

Let us look at the prophecy of Jeremiah 49:34–39:

> *The word of the* Lord *that came to Jeremiah the prophet against Elam in the beginning of the reign of Zedekiah king of Judah, saying: Thus saith the* Lord *of hosts; Behold, I will break the bow of Elam, the chief of their might. And upon Elam will I bring the four winds from the four quarters of heaven, and will scatter them toward all those winds; and there shall be no more nation whither the outcasts of Elam shall not come. For I will cause Elam to be dismayed before their enemies, and before them that seek their life: and I will bring evil upon*

---

39. Benjamin Netanyahu, "Netanyahu's 2024 Address to Congress," Ha'aretz, Accessed on August 22, 2024, https://haaretz.com

them, even my fierce anger, saith the LORD; and I will send the sword after them, till I have consumed them: And I will set my throne in Elam, and will destroy from thence the king and the princes, saith the LORD. But it shall come to pass in the latter days, that I will bring again the captivity of Elam, saith the LORD.

In this prophecy of Jeremiah, he has been giving a prophecy of the coming destruction of many of Israel's enemies, called the Prophecy of the Gentiles (Jer. 46:1). In this section (Jeremiah 46–51), Jeremiah is foretelling the coming defeat of several enemies of Israel, including Egypt, Philistia, Moab, Ammon, Damascus, Edom, Kedar and Hazor, Elam, and Babylon. These judgments are prophesied together as a group, but the timing of fulfillment and the judgment or destruction of each nation is individual and unique.

Jeremiah begins the prophecy with Egypt and moves from west to east, coming to Elam and then Babylon. The most forceful destruction and powerful derision from God was reserved for Babylon, Israel's most prominent enemy at the time.

Elam is an ancient nation that sits across the Persian Gulf from Babylon in the northeastern corner of the area. It covers today's southwestern section of Iran and is divided from the rest of the country by a mountain range. This area is today of strategic importance being the source of water for the country, as well as the location of three nuclear reactors and centers of scientific testing for Iran.

The ancient nation of Elam was a nation that was famed for its warfare with archery like the Scythians (early Russians) and Assyrians. It was earlier conquered by Assyria, later threatened by Babylon, assimilated into the Medo-Persian Empire, and then conquered by Alexander the Great.

In this prophecy, Jeremiah tells of breaking the bow of Elam, the chief of their might, which would be overcoming their military. He says God will scatter the people of Elam from the four winds of heaven across the entire world to the extent that there is no nation to which the people of Elam will not come.

God will send the sword after them until they have been consumed. He will set His throne in their midst, meaning the Lord will personally supervise this judgment as "the Lord Himself will sit in judgment on Elam."[40] And God will destroy their king and princes, meaning He will overcome their political leaders and establish a change in their rule of government.

Finally, in the latter days, He will "bring again the captivity of Elam," meaning God will restore the nation and people of Elam in the Millennium.

Two Views of the Timing of Elam's Fulfillment

The difficulty of studying this prophecy is the question of when it would be fulfilled and scholars are varied in their opinion.

Bill Salus believes that the Elam fulfillment is future and that the entire text has yet to be fulfilled. "In my estimation, Jeremiah 49:34–39 remains entirely unfulfilled and is a stand-alone prophecy, (meaning it is not a part of the wars in Psalm 83 or Ezekiel 38 and 39.)"[41]

Salus believes the entire prophecy is future because he believes the following events:

> There is a severe disaster caused by the Lord's fierce anger (Jer. 49:37), an apparent humanitarian crisis

---

40. Charles L. Feinberg, "Jeremiah," *The Expositor's Bible Commentary*, Gen. Ed. Frank E. Gaebelein, vol. 6 (Grand Rapids, MI: Zondervan, 1986), p. 671.

41. Bill Salus, *Nuclear Showdown in Iran: Revealing the Ancient Prophecy of Elam*, (Las Quinta, CA: Prophecy Depot Ministries, 2014), p. 65.

arises that necessitates a worldwide scattering of the indigenous population of the Elamites/Iranians (Jer. 49:36), there is an utter and complete destruction of Elam by its enemies (Jer. 49:37), and a destroying of the rulers (kings and the princes), which creates a political power vacuum that the Lord fills by setting His throne in the territory (Jer. 49:38).[42]

In this *first view* of Jeremiah 49, Salus contends that the destruction of Elam would be in modern times by military means as God "will send the sword after them." He believes that the entire prophecy has a future fulfillment and he uses modern details to explain the text.

Iran has built three nuclear reactors in the ancient area of Elam, and this includes the Bushehr nuclear reactor, the first one built by Iran which became fully functional in 2010.

In Dr. Reagan's review of Salus' view, he tells us:

It is at this point that Salus begins applying the prophecy to current times. He argues that the prophecy will most likely be fulfilled through an Israeli attack that will destroy the nuclear reactor, and that attack will lead to the Psalm 83 War of Annihilation aimed at Israel.

The destruction of the nuclear reactor would produce such a heavy release of radiation that all the people in the area would flee. This would be the beginning of the worldwide dispersion of the Elamite people as prophesied in verse 16.[43]

In many of Salus's interpretations, he consistently refers to the Israeli Defense Forces (the IDF) as the main object

---

42. Bill Salus, "Has the Prophecy of Elam in Jeremiah 49:34–39 Been Historically Fulfilled?" Prophecy Depot Ministries, Accessed on July 20, 2024, https://prophecydepotministries.net.

43. David R. Reagan, 9 Wars of the End Times.

that brings God's judgment, uses modern interpretations of the verses, sees them fitting into current events, and explains these prophecies as having future fulfillment.

He sometimes uses fanciful concepts in modern times to explain his view. For instance, Salus believes that an Israeli attack on an Iranian nuclear reactor will start the Psalm 83 war, although there is no clear evidence of these details in the text. Perhaps because of the scattering of the people, he supposes that it occurs because the crisis of nuclear radiation would cause people to flee. But this event is simply not clearly detailed in the text.

Salus sees this conflict as the first of several wars with Israel that happens before the Rapture, followed by the Psalm 83 war, and the destruction of Damascus, which he believes will happen before the Rapture and the Russian invasion of Israel.

On the other hand, famed author and Bible prophecy expert Dr. Mark Hitchcock sees the fulfillment of the prophecy of Elam in ancient times through Nebuchadnezzar. This has been the view of commentators for many centuries and this second view is the classic view of Bible scholars. Dr. Hitchcock tells us: "Other than the final verse of Jeremiah 49, dealing with Elam's final restoration, the context of Elam's destruction leads me to conclude this is referring to the historical destruction of Elam in the distant past, not a future judgment of the modern nation of Iran."[44]

In his YouTube broadcast, Dr. Hitchcock specifies his answer that Nebuchadnezzar will be the hand of God's judgment. He says, "The destruction of Elam took place in the reign of King Nebuchadnezzar."[45]

When referring to this passage, Dr. Andy Woods agrees with Dr. Hitchcock saying, "It keeps saying Nebuchadnezzar

---

44. Mark Hitchcock, *Showdown with Iran*, (Emanate Books, 2020), pp. 145–146.
45. Mark Hitchcock, *Marking the Times* Episode 96, January 20, 2020.

you know over and over again in that section so that's a prophecy that was fulfilled back in the sixth century."[46]

Dr. John Walvoord, the esteemed late president of Dallas Theological Seminary, also saw a connection between the destruction of Kedar and Hazor by the Babylonians and the destruction of Elam. Dr. Walvoord said: "A brief prophecy concerning Kedar and Hazor is contained in Jeremiah 49:28–33. It is a prediction of judgment upon them at the hands of Nebuchadnezzar king of Babylon. A similar judgment is pronounced upon Elam in Jeremiah 49:34–39."[47] However, Dr. Walvoord modified his view of Elam and later said:

> The prophecy concerning Elam referred to an area east of Babylon, known today as Iran. The destruction of Elam was described as breaking her bow, for, like Kedar, Elam was noted for archery. The complete destruction of Elam does not seem to have been fulfilled in history and may have its final chapter in the future in connection with judgments at the second coming of Christ. Elam was promised, however, restoration (v. 39).[48]

Dr. David Reagan agrees that this Elam prophecy was fulfilled in history. He gives a more in-depth review of the text and tells us:

> I respectfully disagree [with Salus's view] for several reasons. First is the context of Jeremiah's prophecy. In chapter 49, he is prophesying about immediate judgments God is going to place on Ammon (verse 1), Edom (verse 7), Damascus (verse 23), Kedar and Hazor (verse 28) and Elam (verse 34).

---

46. Andy Woods, *Middle East Meltdown* # 26, August 7, 2022.
47. https://walvoord.com/book/export/html/318.
48. John F. Walvoord, *Every Prophecy of the Bible*, (Colorado Springs, CO: Chariot Victor Publishing, 1999), p. 151.

When he comes to Elam, he does not indicate in any way that the prophecy will happen in a timing different from the other nations mentioned. There is no indication that it will happen in the end times.

Salus argues that its end-time setting is mentioned in the last verse of the prophecy where it says, *"But it will be in the last days that I will return the fortunes of Elam"* (verse 39 NLT). But this verse applies only to the re-establishment of the nation of Elam and the regathering of the Elamites to their homeland. Jeremiah does not apply it to the whole prophecy.

Thus, I believe the first part of the prophecy (verses 35–37) has already been fulfilled in history.[49]

Elam in Ezekiel 32

Bill Salus also uses a related passage from Ezekiel 32 to bolster his view of Jeremiah 49 as a future prophecy for Elam fulfilled in the time of modern Iran. Jeremiah was prophesying about Elam in about 596 BC about the time of the Babylonian invasions of Israel in 605, 597, and 586 BC. Ezekiel's prophecy of Elam was given in 585 BC, about twelve years after Jeremiah's prophetic word.

Interestingly, Bill Salus sees this Ezekiel prophecy as a separate prophecy about Elam that describes current events today, such as using the reference in verse 24 that says, "terror in the land of the living" to apply as a reference to Iran's current terrorist activities today.[50]

But Dr. Hitchcock notes with great insight, "However, in the immediate context, this phrase is used of Assyria (32:23), Meshech and Tubal (32:24), and ... the Sidonians (32:30). Elam is in no way singled out for its terrorizing

---

49. David R. Reagan, *9 Wars of the End Times*, pp. 150.
50. Bill Salus, "Nuclear Iran: Are Ezekiel 38 (Persia) and Jeremiah 49 (Elam) the Same Prophecy?" Prophecy Depot, April 30, 2018.

actions. This doesn't refer to current Iranian terrorism, but to what those nations did in the past." Dr. Hitchcock then explains the Ezekiel 32 passage and shows conclusively why this cannot be a prophecy of future modern fulfillment.

As with Jeremiah 49, I believe the context refers to a past historical judgment of that nation, not an end-time prophecy. The mention of Elam in Ezekiel is in a broader context related to the impending fall of Egypt. Ezekiel 32 is the prophet's sixth prophecy against Egypt. The main point in Ezekiel 32 is that Egypt will be utterly destroyed and that her leader, Pharaoh, and her slain soldiers will descend into Sheol or the underworld.

He [Ezekiel] lists several other mighty nations who have fallen and whose armies will be waiting in the nether world when Pharaoh and her defeated army arrive. The waiting nations he mentions are: Assyria (modern Iraq), Elam (modern Iran), Meshech and Tubal (modern Turkey), and Sidon (modern Lebanon).

In this setting, Ezekiel is unmistakably referring to defeated Elamites in his own day who were already in the grave, waiting for the arrival of the ancient Egyptians. Ezekiel's reference to Elamite soldiers who had already died precludes this prophecy finding fulfillment in the end of days.

How could modern Iranian soldiers be waiting in the underworld for Egyptians who were destroyed more than two and a half millennia ago? This simply doesn't make any sense.[51]

Ezekiel 32 is clearly a prophecy of judgment for Egypt. Notice who it addresses in verse 2, *"Son of man, take up a lamentation for Pharaoh king of Egypt ..."* and the other

---

51. Mark Hitchcock, *Showdown with Iran*, pp. 146–147.

nations that are mentioned are people previously judged and waiting in death for the Egyptian pharaoh and army. The instrument of God's judgment is also mentioned in this chapter in verse 11, *"For thus saith the Lord GOD; The sword of the king of Babylon shall come upon thee."* This is obviously King Nebuchadnezzar.

As a result, in *this second view* of Jeremiah 49 and Ezekiel 32, the prophecy of judgment for Elam was fulfilled in history by Nebuchadnezzar. He is referred to as the instrument of God's judgment in Ezekiel 32:11; the Elamites were judged and killed after the judgment of Jeremiah 49 and twelve years later, they are waiting in death for the Egyptians. Nebuchadnezzar is the person named in the context of both passages. Because of the details and context of the passage, this past fulfillment is conclusively the best interpretation of Jeremiah 49.

However, all of these Bible interpreters agree that there is a future plan for the return of the Elamite people and that their fortune would be changed into a blessing. *"But it shall come to pass in the latter days, that I will bring again the captivity of Elam, saith the LORD"* (Jer. 49:39). This will happen after Armageddon when God will re-establish the various peoples of the world such as the people of Elam and return them to their historic homeland and they will serve the Lord in the Millennium.

Thus, we see that Iran is a constant threat to Israel, but there is no certain biblical prophecy that details a future war only with Israel and Iran. While there could be such a war, it is not mentioned in the Bible. Yet, is there a biblical prophecy for a war with Syria and Israel in the future?

CHAPTER SIX

THE POSSIBLE ISRAELI WAR WITH SYRIA

Damascus, Syria, is one of the oldest continually inhabited cities of the world and it was mentioned in Genesis 15:2. Abraham's trusted servant, Eliezer, was from Damascus. Damascus and the area of Syria are mentioned in Isaiah 17, Jeremiah 49, and Zephaniah 2. The area of Syria was also controlled by Assyria iñ ancient times and it is often mentioned in the Bible.

There has been historic fighting between the two nations of Israel and Syria throughout history with Tiglath-Pileser III, Shalmaneser V, Sargon II, and Sennacherib. The Assyrian Empire was the political entity that captured the northern kingdom of Israel in 722 BC.

And there is current tension today, with different religions and a history of racial tension and animosity between the Jews and Arabs. Yet, is there a real possibility of this escalating into a future war with Israel and Syria?

Currently, the terrorist organization Hezbollah is operating in Lebanon and Syria. The country of Lebanon is being used as a base of operations for Hezbollah. There are about one hundred thousand missiles located near the border of Israel and aimed at her north from these two countries of Syria and Lebanon. With an almost daily barrage of missiles, about ten thousand missiles have been shot from this northern area of Syria and Lebanon into Israel since the October 7 attack by Hamas.

There is a constant attack on Israel from this northern region. Almost every night, Israel sends fighter jets to attack these missile installations, especially in Lebanon. Dr. Jimmy DeYoung Jr. said,

> The IDF is waiting and as soon as they get the green light, they can be across the border in minutes and everybody is prepared for a northern invasion of Lebanon. You've got Hezbollah in Lebanon and you've got Hezbollah all along the northern border between Israel and Syria. The Israeli air force is attacking on a nightly basis weapons depots in Lebanon to limit the collateral damage. They are ready for a ground invasion and waiting for the word to go.[52]

After nearly 12 months of Israeli-Hezbollah conflict, Israel invaded Southern Lebanon on October 1, 2024. Hezbollah had joined with the Hamas attack on Israel's northern border and Israel responded with an aerial bombing campaign, an attack on pagers and electronic devices and the assassination of Hezbollah leader Hassan Nasrallah and others. Also, small covert raids uncovered Hezbollah tunnels, weaponry and invasion plans of northern Israeli villages similar to the earlier Hamas mass murder of Israelis on October 7, 2023.

Israel pushed Hezbollah to the Litani River and advised civilians to evacuate southern Lebanon. Hezbollah continued to launch rockets and Iran launched at least 181 missiles to attack Israel and they both tried to assassinate Israeli Prime Minister Netanyahu and his wife on October 19. Although a cease-fire began on November 27, unrest continues in the area.

Meanwhile, after the fall of the Assad regime in Syria, Israel invaded the buffer zone of Syria on December 8, destroyed Syria's navy, air force, and weapons facilities

---

52. Jimmy DeYoung Jr., "Israel Continues Under Fire," *Crosstalk*, vcy.org/crosstalk/2024/09/09/Israel-continues-under-fire/

including chemical weapons such as mustard and VX gas and stockpiles of Scud missiles, and destroyed Iranian arms smuggling routes in Syria.

The threat of Iran has been reduced. Iran was using proxy terrorist groups such as Hamas, Hezbollah, the Houthis and the navy and air force of Syria to attack Israel. Their primary hope of attack was their ballistic missiles but only one of the 181 missiles struck Israel and most were destroyed by Israel's Iron Dome. Iran's nuclear weapons program is hidden deep underground and is threatened to be destroyed by both Israel and the US.

While the threat of Iran and Syria has been greatly decreased, Turkey has risen to try to take control of Syria, and her dictator, Erdogan, wants to be the prime leader of the Middle East and reestablish an Ottoman Empire. So, the power struggle against Israel is constantly changing.

Because of the current unrest in Syria, and the past use of Syria by Iran, Russia, and even North Korea to build nuclear plants, and to train and equip terrorists, all aimed at overcoming Israel, many people wonder: Is there a prophetic future with war and judgment mentioned for Syria?

The Destruction of Damascus and the Conquest of Syria

The Bible mentions the coming judgment of God on many nations and the Bible also tells of coming judgment on Damascus and Syria. Again, there is a difference of opinion on the timing of this judgment of Damascus and this study will consider the fulfillment of Isaiah 17. Note especially Isaiah 17:1-3.

> *The burden of Damascus. Behold, Damascus is taken away from being a city, and it shall be a ruinous heap. The cities of Aroer are forsaken: they shall be for flocks,*

which shall lie down, and none shall make them afraid. The fortress also shall cease from Ephraim, and the kingdom from Damascus, and the remnant from Syria: they shall be as the glory of the children of Israel, saith the Lord of hosts.

There are three primary views of this passage. In the first view, Joel Rosenberg gives a description of the passage and believes that this passage has a very near future fulfillment, possibly before the Rapture. He explains this passage:

> When viewed together, we can say the following about the prophecies of Damascus found in Isaiah 17 and Jeremiah 49:
>
> 1. The prophecies refer to a divine judgment by God against the city of Damascus.
> 2. The prophecies refer to the utter, catastrophic destruction of Damascus.
> 3. Both are eschatological passages, referring to End Time events that have yet to occur.
>   A. Isaiah's prophecy was given to him in 715 BC, well after the conquering of Damascus in 732 by Tiglath-Pileser.
>   B. Likewise, Jeremiah's ministry occurred between 626 BC and 685 BC, long after Tiglath-Pileser conquered Damascus in 732 BC.
> 4. We cannot be certain when these judgments will happen, and the prophecies will be fulfilled.
>   A. They could come to pass before, during, or after the War of Gog and Magog (Ezekiel 38–39), before, during, or after the Rapture, or before or during the Tribulation.
>   B. It is possible that the prophecies could come

to pass in the not-too-distant future. But they certainly will come to pass before the Second Coming of Christ (the "Day of the Lord").[53]

Bill Salus and others hold a similar view and see other things in the passage happening in a modern time. He believes that an Israeli nuclear strike on Syria will cause a war that will result in Israel destroying Damascus, leaving it in ruins and uninhabited.

In *this first view,* Rosenberg and Salus see a future fulfillment of the destruction of Damascus in the very near future, possibly before the Rapture and they both tie it together with Jeremiah 49. We dealt earlier with the past fulfillment of Jeremiah 49.

Rosenberg gives a detailed analysis of Isaiah 17 and bases his view primarily on the dating of the passage in relation to the destruction in 732 BC and his view that the passages are eschatological (that they have future fulfillment).

Dr. Hitchcock deftly answers these two points. First, is the passage eschatological?

> I agree that many parts of Isaiah 13–24 are eschatological, but not everything. Isaiah 16:14 refers to the destruction of Moab "within three years." Isaiah 21:16 says, "Within a year, according to the years of an hireling, and all the glory of Kedar shall fail." These prophecies clearly have a near fulfillment in view.[54]

Thus, part of this section is future, and part of this section is specifically mentioned as having fulfillment "within three years" or "within a year." Context is vitally important as Dr.

---

53. Joel C. Rosenberg, "Notes on the Future of Damascus According to Bible Prophecy," Accessed on July 24, 2024, https://www.joelrosenberg.com

54. Mark Hitchcock, *Showdown with Iran,* p. 157.

Hitchcock reminds us.

Next, he skillfully deals with the timing of the giving of the prophecy in Isaiah 17.

> One point that Rosenberg makes is that Isaiah 17 was prophesied in 715 BC, so it can't be a prophecy about the destruction of Damascus in 732 BC by the Assyrians. He gets the date from Isaiah 14:28, which refers to the "year that king Ahaz died" which was 715 BC.
>
> However, this is the date for the oracle against the Philistines in Isaiah 14:29–32, but there's no evidence it's the date for the oracle against Damascus three chapters later. So, there's nothing in the context to preclude the Assyrian destruction of Damascus in 732 BC from being the fulfillment of Isaiah's prophecy.[55]

In this second view, Dr. Hitchcock believes that Isaiah 17 had a historical fulfillment through the destruction of Damascus by the Assyrian army of Tiglath-Pileser in 732 BC. He bases this view upon his understanding of the context of Isaiah 17. He says:

> My main reason for viewing Isaiah 17 as fulfilled in the past is the immediate context. In the verses just before Isaiah 17:1, Isaiah prophesies the destruction of ancient Moab and says it will occur "within three years" (Isaiah 16:14). This clearly sets the date of the oracle in the very near future.
>
> Then, in the final verses of Isaiah 17, the prophet looks ahead to the total destruction of the Assyrian army in 701 BC in one night (Isaiah 17:12–14). This was fulfilled in 701 BC when the army of Sennacherib, numbering 185,000, was killed by one angel on a single night as they camped in the land of Judah (Isaiah 37:36).

---

55. Mark Hitchcock, *Showdown with Iran*, p. 184.

Since the context before Isaiah 17:1–2 is a near future fulfillment and the context after it is also a near fulfillment, it would be strange for Isaiah 17:1–2 to have a distinct fulfillment in the end times.[56]

Thus, in *this second view*, Isaiah 17 is seen to have a past fulfillment in the Assyrian destruction of Damascus in 732 BC. While he holds some sections of Isaiah to be eschatological (or future), he believes the destruction of Damascus had a past fulfillment.

A third view of this passage is also sometimes mentioned by solid Bible scholars. Founder and president of the Pre-Trib Research Center, Dr. Thomas Ice sees this area of Isaiah to be primarily future in fulfillment with some sections fulfilled in the past. This is echoed by other Bible commentators.

Harry Bultema tells us:

> The judgment that will strike Damascus is that it will be no longer a city but a ruinous heap. This prediction has yet to be completely fulfilled, for in Jeremiah's day it was a flourishing city, and even today is said to be the oldest city in the world (c.f. Genesis 15:2 where Damascus is already mentioned).
>
> According to 2 Kings 16:9, Tiglath-Pileser captured it and killed its king Rezin, but he did not make it a heap. This chapter, however, points to the terrible end time of the Great Tribulation when all the cities of the Gentiles will fall including Damascus.[57]

Dr. Thomas Ice noted that Damascus had been captured but not completely destroyed numerous times in her history.

---

56. Ibid., pp. 157–158.
57. Harry Bultema, *Commentary on Isaiah* (Grand Rapids: Kregel Publishers, 1981), p. 184.

Dr. Hitchcock responds by saying that Isaiah does not say that the city would never be rebuilt or inhabited again. But the context tells us this is now a ruin that is a dwelling for animals not to fear because there is no presence of mankind (verse 2).

Dr. Ice also noted that John Nelson Darby also sees this as a future event, rather than being fulfilled in the past. Darby says:

> I do not see how this is possible, in all this part of Isaiah, from chapter 13 and even before, not to see that the Spirit of God is taking up the great plan of God and speaking of future coming events, but taking hold of present ones as an occasion, and that connected with the government of God then, which will be fully displayed at the end.
>
> Note Damascus was taken by the King of Assyria in the reign of Ahaz, but all this is evidently in the latter days. Moab, however, suffers first from the heathen.[58]

Although these commentators see a past fulfillment of some of these passages, they see the destruction of Damascus as a future event. It is interesting to remember that Dr. Hitchcock has also seen some of this section of Isaiah as future, yet their views of the judgment of Damascus are different. He sees a past fulfillment while they look to a future fulfillment.

The crux of the question is: Which part of the prophecy is future? Then Dr. Ice asks the question: When is the future destruction of Damascus? He finds the answer in the context of Isaiah 17.

> The final section of the chapter gives us a perspective as to when in the future Damascus will be removed from

---

58. John Nelson Darby, *Notes and Comments on Scripture*, 7 volumes (Sunbury, PA: Believers Bookshelf, reprint 1971), vol. IV, pp. 35–36.

being a city. Verses twelve through fourteen say, "Alas, the uproar of many peoples who roar like the roaring of the seas, and the rumbling of nations who rush on like the rumbling of mighty waters! The nations rumble on like the rumbling of many waters, but He will rebuke them and they will flee far away, and be chased like chaff in the mountains before the wind. At eveningtime, behold there is terror! Before morning they are no more. Such will be the portion of those who plunder us, and the lot of those who pillage us."

This passage is similar to other passages that speak of the judgment of the nations at Armageddon (compare Joel 3:1–7; Matt. 24:29–31; Rev. 16:14, 19:11–21). Therefore, it could not happen in our day or before the rapture. Instead, it appears to be an event that will occur at the end of the seven-year tribulation as the Lord not only judges and destroys Damascus, but all Israel's historic enemies that surround her.

If one examines the broader context of Isaiah 17 and takes account of the section where it is located, it becomes clear that it is a section in which the Lord prophesies judgment upon all the Gentile nations that have opposed Israel. This all happens at the end of the tribulation in conjunction with the second coming of Christ to the Earth.

The judgment of the nation's section (Isaiah 13–23) is then followed by a condemnation of the world section (Isaiah 24–35). These judgments will clearly take place at the end of the tribulation when all the nations are gathered together against Israel at Armageddon. In the list of the nations in Isaiah to be judged, Babylon is first on the list. Babylon will be wiped out, never to be inhabited again, toward the end of the tribulation (Rev. 17–18). Note the section on Damascus in Isaiah.

Damascus will be destroyed at the end of the tribulation.

Thus, in *this third view,* taking into account the earlier destruction and conquest of Damascus, as well as the context of Isaiah 17, Damascus was conquered in 732 BC but never made a ruinous heap and was continually rebuilt and inhabited. There were past judgments for Moab and others, but the context of the end of the chapter tells us that the total destruction of Damascus and the judgment of the nations will occur at the end of the Tribulation period during the Campaign of Armageddon.

Thus, the war of Psalm 83 and this passage of Isaiah 17 will be fulfilled at Armageddon. The passages of Jeremiah 49 and Ezekiel 32 had a historical fulfillment and are pictures in type of the coming judgment of the Gentile nations at Armageddon. There are no wars specified to occur before the Rapture and these conflicts were fulfilled in history (Jer. 49, Ezek. 32) or will be fulfilled at Armageddon (Ps. 83 and Isa. 17).

Are These Wars Related to the Russian Invasion of Israel?

Why are people looking for multiple wars before the Rapture and before the Tribulation? Phillip Goodman sees the underlying assumptions by others that bring an incorrect future speculation about Israel's wars being fulfilled before the Rapture and Tribulation. He looks into details about the Gog and Magog war and compares and contrasts it with Psalm 83.

Goodman notes the reasons speculators have suggested the Psalm 83 war precludes the Russian Invasion of Israel. Let us answer each objection with biblical clarity.

1. The nations listed in Psalm 83 are not named among the nations in the Magog invasion (Ezek. 38:1–7).

Therefore, they cannot be part of that event and must represent another event.

These researchers propose that Psalm 83 mentions *the inner ring* of nations around Israel (Palestinians and Jordan, Saudi Arabia, Syria, Lebanon, Arabs of the Sinai area, Arabs of the Gaza strip, and Iraq) while the Magog Invasion includes *an outer ring* of nations (Russia, Iran, Sudan, Libya, Turkey, Gomer [probably Turkey] and they are joined by "many peoples" (Ezek. 39:1–5). So, they are looking for a war that involves the *inner ring* of nations.

Yet, since the invading nations of the Magog Invasion are all Muslim nations except Russia, it stands to reason that the "many peoples" could include the other nearby inner ring of Muslim nations with the outer ring. So, logically, all these nations could be involved in the Magog invasion. The text does not mention them but includes "many peoples" so it is not possible to be definitive.

In the War of Armageddon, the inner nations are also mentioned in many Bible passages. Joel 3 mentions Tyre (South Lebanon), Sidon (Lebanon), Philistia (Gaza), Egypt, and Edom (Jordan). Isaiah 11 mentions Philistia, Edom, Moab (Jordan), Ammon (Jordan), Egypt, and Assyria (Syria, Iraq). And Zechariah 14 mentions the inner ring of "surrounding nations" and Egypt. Thus, Armageddon will include the inner nations and other nations of the world. Consequently, this is a better answer for the Psalm 83 war.

2. A prerequisite for the Magog invasion is that Israel must be "dwelling securely" in the land. Because of the danger of Israel's surrounding nations, they must attack and defeat them to dwell securely.

This view presupposes that Israel is dwelling unsecured. Israel was in constant danger in her diaspora, and her people were persecuted and killed during most of the last two thousand years. However, after the infamous Holocaust, Israel gained their own homeland and built a land of unwalled villages where the people can dwell in relative security, so Israel views itself today as "dwelling securely."

3. As a result of this Psalm 83 conquest of the entire Middle East (the Sinai Peninsula, Gaza, Lebanon, Jordan, Syria, and Iraq), Israel will capture and secure boundaries for themselves across the entire Arab lands promised to Israel by God in Genesis 15:18–21. This would include all the lands from the Mediterranean Sea to the Euphrates River. Some researchers believe they must capture the entire Middle East before the Rapture and before the Magog invasion.

When is the timing for the capture of the Psalm 83 nations? Here, Philip Goodman brings a solid biblical answer.

> In Isaiah 11:11–15, Israel "swoops down" and captures the Psalm 83 nations. The passage says that this occurs when the Jews return a "second time" to the land of Israel. Is this second return the one of 1948? If so, Israel could conquer the Middle East nations at any time, as the Psalm 83 theory proposes. But this passage is actually describing events when Jesus returns at the end of the Great Tribulation.[59]

Another solid Bible scholar, Dr. Arno Fruchtenbaum, has informed us:

> The regathering spoken of in this passage is the one in faith in preparation for the Millennial Kingdom. This regathering in faith is specifically stated to be a second international regathering. The first regathering is the one which will be in preparation for judgment (1948

---

59. Philip Goodman, *The Psalm 83 Prophecy*, (Tulsa, OK: Bible Prophecy as Written, Sept./Oct.2013), p. 8.

to the Tribulation), the second regathering will be in preparation for blessing.⁶⁰

Goodman then sees the timing of Psalm 83 and Isaiah 11 happening together: "Therefore, the events of Isaiah 11, including the conquest of the Psalm 83 nations, take place at the time of the Second Coming of Christ in preparation for the Millennial Kingdom."⁶¹

With this telling insight into the theory of pre-Rapture wars, it is obvious that the pre-Rapture interpreters such as Salus, Rosenberg, and others are looking for an almost complete takeover of the entire Middle East by Israel. They believe Israel must conquer these nations to bring the Magog invasion and to cause Russia and her cohorts to want to come to Israel to take a spoil. These commentators see this as an attempt by Russia and her allies to get the oil-rich land from Israel.

Yet, it is clear that Israel will not possess the greater Middle East until after the Tribulation period. Although she was promised the land as part of Abraham's promise from God in Genesis 15 and the Land Covenant amplified this promise to Israel, she will not possess the entire land until the time of the Millennium.

Dr. Fruchtenbaum again gives great insight: "Following the regeneration of Israel at the Second Coming of Christ, God will fully carry out the Abrahamic Covenant concerning the land. ... For the first time in Israel's history, she will possess all the Promised Land."⁶²

As a result, we can see the primary reason for speculation about wars mentioned in the Bible is to deal with details of the Magog invasion and the supposition that

---

60. Arno Fruchtenbaum, *Israelology*, p. 718.
61. Philip Goodman, *The Psalm 83 Prophecy*, p. 8.
62. Arnold Fruchtenbaum, *The Footsteps of Messiah*, pp. 431, 438.

Israel will possess all the land of the Middle East, possibly before the Rapture.

Yet, we have seen conclusively that these suppositions have been answered and that there is no war mentioned in the Bible to occur before the Rapture. And Israel will not possess their Promised Land until after the return of Christ at Armageddon.

There is no event mentioned in the Bible as a prerequisite to the Rapture, or as an earlier requirement for the Rapture to happen, because it is an imminent event. The Rapture could happen at any moment.

While future Middle East wars with Israel may occur, the biblical wars have either already been fulfilled in history (Jer. 49; Ezek. 32) or they will be fulfilled in the Tribulation period (Psalm 83 and Isaiah 17 will occur with Armageddon.)

And because of the confusion about the timing of events such as when Israel possesses their land, there is sometimes confusion about their related events such as the individual judgments of the nations. Yet, when we see these events in their biblical chronology, we can be assured about the timing of other events such as the timing of military conflicts.

Thus, there are only four future wars for Israel and the Earth mentioned in the Bible: the Magog invasion of Israel (Ezek. 38–39), the World War I of the Tribulation beginning with the second Seal Judgment of Revelation 6:3–4, the middle Tribulation War in Daniel 11 (World War II of the Tribulation), and the Campaign of Armageddon in Revelation 19 (World War III of the Tribulation). All other wars and conflicts mentioned in the Bible have already been fulfilled in history or will be folded into and occur with these other conflicts.

CHAPTER SEVEN

THE PARTICIPANTS OF THE GOG AND MAGOG WAR

The Bible mentions a time when a great number of nations come to attack Israel. This will include nations from Europe, Central Asia, and Africa and they will be destroyed supernaturally by the Lord. This prophesied war has never happened in history, so it must be a future war for Israel.

All Bible commentators who believe in a literal future for Israel see a coming war described in Ezekiel 38–39 as the Gog and Magog war. This is also often referred to as the future Russian and multinational invasion of Israel. We must first identify the attacking and protesting nations.

Who Is Involved in this Invasion of Israel?

There are nine regions with multiple countries that make up a multinational confederacy of nations that attack Israel. When the ancient names are determined to match modern nations, it is understood that eleven modern nations will join in a coalition to attack Israel in this invasion.

The list of nations is given in Ezekiel 38:1–6:

And the word of the LORD came unto me, saying, Son of man, set thy face against Gog, the land of Magog, the chief prince of Meshech and Tubal, and prophecy against him, And say, Thus saith the Lord GOD; Behold, I am against thee, O Gog, the chief prince of Meshech and Tubal: And I will turn thee back, and put hooks into thy jaws, and I will bring thee forth, and all thine army, horses and horsemen, all of them clothed with all sorts of armour, even a great company with bucklers and shields, all of them handling swords: Persia, Ethiopia, and Libya with them; all of them with shield and helmet: Gomer, and all his bands; the house of Togarmah of the north quarters, and all his bands: and many people with thee.

In this prophecy, the Lord God addresses a person named Gog. He stands against Gog, the leader of the multinational confederacy, and He is against the entire invasion of nations. The name Gog refers to the title of the leader, similar to the title of a king, general, or president, and it is not his actual name.

While the word — Gog — is the title of the leader of the invasion, his identification will not be known until the time of the invasion. Whoever is the leader of this coalition of nations at the invading time will be Gog. About his identity, Dr. Hitchcock tells us: "The name *Gog* means "high, supreme, a height, or a high mountain." The way the name is used in Ezekiel 38–39 certainly reveals that Gog is a person, not a place. Gog is a person from the land of Magog who is the prince or ruler of Rosh, Meshech, and Tubal."[63]

The Lord will put into Gog's mind the desire for the invasion of Israel and will influence his will as God had earlier done with Pharaoh during the time of Moses. In each instance, God is demonstrating His power, sovereignty, and will over the nations. By putting Israel in distress, and yet saving her from ultimate destruction, the Lord is able to turn the Jewish people to believe in God and to return to Him. And God is also demonstrating His authority and control of the nations.

Gog comes from "the north parts" (Ezek. 38:15). Ezekiel 39:2 tells us, *"And I will turn thee back, and leave but the sixth part of thee, and will cause thee to come up from the north parts, and will bring thee upon the mountains of Israel."*

---

63. Mark Hitchcock, *After the Empire,* (Wheaton, IL: Tyndale House Publishers, 1994), p. 17.

In some translations, this phrase is rendered from "the remotest parts of the north." Thus, this Gog would come from an area far north of Israel. The Caucasus Mountains are due north of Israel between the Black and Caspian seas in the former Soviet Union.

Dr. Hitchcock has done the most research in this area and again gives great insight: "Interestingly, the word *Caucasus* means 'Gog's Fort.' *Gog* and *Chasan* ('fort') are the two words from which the word *Caucasus* is derived. This mountain range is called 'Gog's Fort!'"[64]

This person comes from "the land of Magog" and is described as the "prince of Rosh, Meshech, and Tubal." These ancient nations are directly related to modern nations today. So, we must next look at: Who is Magog?

Magog

The first nation group mentioned by Ezekiel is Magog. Magog is a region that is seen to join with Rosh, Meshech, Tubal, and other nations. Ezekiel refers to these nations as the nations he knew at this time during the Israelite captivity in Babylon under Nebuchadnezzar, who ruled from 605–562 BC. This first nation is actually a very large region and covers part of Russia and central Asia.

The ancient Jewish historian Josephus informs us, "Magog founded the Magogians, thus named after him, but who by the Greeks are called Scythians."[65] The designation of Scythians can refer in a narrower sense to a territory north of the Black Sea, or in a broad sense, "the word Scythian can designate some of the many tribes in the vast steppes of Russia, stretching from Ukraine in the west to the region of Siberia in the east."[66]

---

64. Ibid., p. 18.
65. Flavius Josephus, *Antiquities of the Jews*, vol. 1, vi, i.
66. Edwin M. Yamauchi, *Foes from the Northern Frontier* (Grand Rapids: Baker Book House, 1982). P. 64.

Throughout their history, these tribes were known as fierce and barbaric fighters. This savagery was so widely known as a danger to the region that the Chinese built the Great Wall of China to keep these people from their land of China. The name of the Great Wall of China in Arabic is *the Wall of Al Magog*.[67]

The Scythians in the time of Ezekiel were divided by the Persians into three groups living in the modern area of Ukraine and stretching throughout the five former central Asian Soviet republics. Dr. Hitchcock again tells us:

> The homeland of the ancient Scythians is inhabited today by the former Soviet republics of Kazakhstan, Kirghizia, Uzbekistan, Turkmenistan, Tajikistan, and Ukraine. All of these former republics, which are now independent nations, are Muslim nations except Ukraine. All the former republics are being courted by their Islamic neighbors — especially by Turkey and Iran.[68]

Thus, Magog is made up of the lower central Asian part of the former Soviet Union as well as Ukraine. Because these central nations except Ukraine are Muslim, it would be easier to draw them into a coalition with other nations to attack Israel, having had a long history of animosity between the two religious groups.

Rosh

The next nation mentioned by Ezekiel is Rosh. This nation's name is derived from the Hebrew word that is translated as "chief prince" in Ezekiel 38:2 in the King James Version, Revised Standard Version, the New American Bible, and the New International Version.

---

67. Ed Hindson, Tim LaHaye, *Global Warning: Are We on the Brink of World War III?* (Eugene, OR: Harvest House Publishers, 2008), p. 129.

68. Mark Hitchcock, *After the Empire*, p. 23.

This word can mean a name or a title. Because of the Hebrew accents in the text, the word has been translated as a title, "the chief prince." But C. F. Keil[69] and Wilhelm Gesenius[70] each state that Rosh mentioned in Ezekiel 38:2–3 and 39:1 denotes a geographical location.

Because of the similar sound of Rosh to Russia, many scholars have concluded that Rosh is Russia. However, a similar-sounding word is not proof that the word Rosh means Russia; this could only be a coincidence. Is there any other evidence?

In ancient history, the Babylonian Chronicle refers to an ancient people in the land of Rasapu,[71] located in Sarmatia, between the Black and Caspian seas sometimes called the Sarmatians of Rosh. The eminent Russian history scholar, George Vernadsky says:

> At the beginning of the fourth century BC another Iranian people, the Sarmatians, began to press upon the Scythians, and by the end of the second-century BC they had occupied the shores of the Black Sea. Among the Sarmatians, one tribe was known as the Rukh-As — "the light (or brilliant) Alans," and it is from this name that Ros or Rus (hence Russia, Russians) presumably derives.[72]

This name of Rosh was eventually applied to the entire area of modern Russia. It is believed that the early Sarmatians became the Russ, and were later called the Russians. They came originally from the area of the countries of central Asia such as Armenia, Georgia, Azerbaijan, Kazakhstan,

---

69. C.F. Keil, "Ezekiel, Daniel," *Commentary on the Old Testament*, trans. James Martin (Grand Rapids: Eerdmans Publishing Company, 1982), p. 159.

70. Wilhelm Gesenius, *Gesenius' Hebrew and Chaldean Lexicon* (Grand Rapids: Eerdmans Publishing Company, 1949), p. 752.

71. Ed Hindson, Tim LaHaye, *Global Warning: Are We on the Brink of World War III?*, p. 134.

72. George Vernadsky, *A History of Russia* (Philadelphia: The Blackiston Company, 1929), pp. 15–16.

Kirghizia, Uzbekistan, Turkmenistan, and Tajikistan and they moved to the area of Ukraine, and later, to the southern and northern parts of Russia.

Today, Russia occupies the area furthest north of Israel and the Russian capital of Moscow lies on a direct line north of Israel. This is the area where the ruler of the coalition originates.

Because of the ancient history of the people of Magog (the Scythians) and Rosh (the Sarmatians) who now are clearly the people of the former Soviet republics (Magog) and Russia (Rosh), we can see a historical connection, as well as a recent connection to the people and know where this leader and army emerge. These nations will join together and then form a coalition of other nations to prepare for the invasion.

Yet, how can the Russians and the former Soviet republics join with the other Arab and Islamic nations? While the Russians have historically fought the Arab people, such as in Afghanistan and Chechnya, today the Central Asian countries of the former Soviet Union are the source of weapons such as rifles, anti-tank weapons, and missiles, and the Russians are the source of much of the scientific work done in the Arab countries for military expansion.

The rich oil reserves of the Middle East have been a source of wealth that the Arab countries have used. This wealth has been the primary motivation to lure the military help of their Russian and Central Asian neighbors. But many of the people of these Arab nations have often continued to live in third-world living conditions while their leadership lives in personal splendor and immense wealth.

Yet, these nations of Russia and the former Soviet republics are also joined in the invasion by allies of other nations. Who are the allies?

Meshech

In Ezekiel 38:2, it mentions "the chief prince of Meshech and Tubal." Sometimes Meshech and Tubal have also been related to modern cities by their similar sound. One commentator believed that these ancient cities were in southern Russia and were the origin of the names of the capital city Moscow, and the city of Tolbolsk which is east of the Ural Mountains of Siberia. Consequently, some researchers view these cities as part of eastern and western Russia.

However, in ancient times Meshech was a trading partner with Tyre of northern Lebanon. By the ninth century BC, the people of Meshech were called the Mushki and were inhabiting Phrygia in northern Anatolia in modern Turkey. Josephus identified them as living in Cappadocia, and they later lived in southeastern and northeastern parts of modern Turkey.[73] Thus, Meshech in Ezekiel is referring to a part of modern Turkey.

Tubal

Although sometimes mistaken as a part of Siberian Russia, Tubal was often historically involved with Meshech and was located in eastern Anatolia. This ancient city-state was also in Cappadocia and they operated together in trade and joined Meshech in fighting the Assyrians in 713 BC.

These two city-states often appear together in Scripture, and they were mentioned together during the reign of the Persian king Cyrus about 500 BC. This leads to the clear understanding that these city-states refer to parts of modern Turkey.

Gomer

The identification of the people of Gomer is the most controversial to determine. The people of Gomer during the time of Ezekiel were the Cimmerians. These ancient

---
73. Flavius Josephus, *Antiquities of the Jews*, vol. 1, pp. vi, i.

people occupied an area in modern Turkey, but some of the people moved north to Bulgaria and it is also believed that some of the people moved to the area of the Danube River and became the Germans.

This has developed into three theories. One view is that the people are the Eastern Europeans such as the Bulgarians and others. According to this view, the Eastern bloc of European nations is Gomer and these nations will join with Russia in the future invasion. This would essentially be an invasion by the former Soviet Union countries with very few allies. This view was especially popular after World War II and continued until the fall of the Soviet Union.

Another view is that Gomer refers to the German people and several Germans have told this author that they came from the line of Gomer, although they did not understand how Germany would ever join Russia to invade Israel. The Jewish Talmud mentions the *Germani* who are believed to be the Germans.

Because there were several tribes of Germans, it is sometimes reasoned that another group of Germanic people outside of Germany would join with Russia. The tribes of Germanic people eventually settled in several countries and exist today in as many as seventeen nations. It is sometimes thought that Germany or one of the other Germanic peoples might join with Russia, although this seems extremely unlikely.

However, the third view is that the term Gomer refers to the Cimmerian people in Turkey. The Cimmerian people originated in the area of modern Ukraine but moved south to eastern Anatolia, and then continued to central and western Anatolia, which is the west-central part of modern Turkey and have occupied most of modern Turkey. Josephus identifies the Gomerites with the Galatians who inhabited central Turkey in his day.[74]

---

74. Ibid.

The Cimmerians were also the people of Gomer in Ezekiel's day. While some of these people did eventually migrate to the area of Bulgaria, the main bloc of the people of Gomer went to Turkey. Thus, the people of Gomer are the people of central and western Turkey today.

Beth-Togarmah

Ezekiel 28:6 mentions, "the house of Togarmah of the north quarters" which is Beth–Togarmah. While some researchers believe that Togarmah refers to the Cossacks in the southern and eastern parts of Russia, others believe that it is Armenia, while another view is that it is Turkey.

In ancient times, Togarmah was the ancient Hittite city of Tegarma in eastern Cappadocia of modern Turkey. The modern nation of Turkey lies north of Israel. Gesenius identified Togarmah as ancient Armenia, which was also in Turkey.[75] Other ancient and historical sources identify Togarmah as Phrygia or other locations, but all of these places are in different areas located inside of modern Turkey.

Persia

Of the nations mentioned in Ezekiel 38–39, the easiest country to identify today is Persia. In ancient times, the kingdom of Persia was allied with Media and was originally the smaller, less powerful country. Together, these nations conquered Babylon under Cyrus but Persia gradually became the main superpower to follow Babylon.

Persia ruled in unquestioned power until defeated by Alexander the Great and the Hellenistic (or Greek) Empire came to rule. However, Persia continued in history under their name until 1935 when it became Iran.

Since the overthrow of the Shah of Iran in 1979, the country went from being an ally of America to becoming one of the centers of terrorism in the world. Led by radical

---
75. Wilhelm Gesenius, *Hebrew and Chaldean Lexicon*, p. 856.

Shiite Muslims, the country has backed terrorism, worked for the downfall of Israel, and in 1992 they acquired two nuclear warheads.

Since that time, they have worked to assemble a huge number of weapons, modernize their military, join with other Muslim nations in their goals, and back Hezbollah, Hamas, Gaza, the Palestinian Authority, and other terrorist groups to bring about the destruction of Israel.

Recently, since the fall of the Soviet Union, Iran has used Soviet scientists to develop their weapons technology and purchased much of Russia's military might. They purchased submarines, and are also modernizing their army and air force to become a major fighting force.[76] It is not difficult to imagine a modern Muslim Iran agreeing to join with Russia in an effort to destroy Israel.

Ethiopia

The name of Ethiopia in Ezekiel 38:5 is sometimes translated as Cush. The Bible refers to two locations for the people of Cush (Gen. 10:6–7; Ezek. 38:5). In the earliest times, they were in western Mesopotamia, in the area of modern Iraq. Nimrod led the people of this area and it is believed by some people that he gave this name to the predecessors of the Babylonians to become the Kassites (or Cushites).[77]

Later, these people moved from Mesopotamia through Arabia to somewhere in Africa and became the black race of people. This has led to a view of various peoples and locations in Africa including the area of Abyssinia, which is modern Ethiopia.

However, the land of Cush was called Nubia by the ancient Greeks and was located directly south and east of

---

76. "Russia–Iran," *Jerusalem*, p. 8.
77. Mark Hitchcock, *After the Empire*, pp. 77.

Egypt.[78] While this name has also been applied to various groups and locations of Africans, it becomes clear from multiple sources that the name used in Ezekiel applies only to Egypt's southern neighbor, which is the nation of Sudan.

Modern Sudan is a Sunni Muslim nation with a militant government that supports terrorism, operates four guerrilla training camps, has ties with Iran and Iraq, has instituted Islamic sharia law, and operates as an Islamic state. The leaders of Sudan want to spread Islam across Africa and the Middle East and bring about a militant Muslim world. It is easy to see how this nation would support a war with Israel.

Libya

Ezekiel 38:5 also mentions the nation by the name of Libya. This name is also translated as Put or Phut in various other versions of the Bible. Although this nation is sometimes interpreted as Somalia, the majority of interpreters see this as Libya.

In ancient history, Nebuchadnezzar did battle with ancient Egypt, progressing as far as Puta, which was the western neighbor of Egypt now known as Libya. Josephus tells us the founder of Libya was Put, and it is identified by Gesenius, Brown-Driver-Briggs, and the Septuagint as the modern nation of Libya.[79]

In ancient times, the country of Libya also included Algeria, Tunisia, Mali, Niger, and northwest Chad, so it is conceivable that this mention of Libya could be applied to only modern Libya or it could also include these other African nations.

In more recent years the nation of Libya was ruled by the radical leader Muammar al-Gadhafi and was responsible

---

78. Pinches, "Cush," in *Bible Encyclopedia*, 2: pp, 708.
79. Mark Hitchcock, *After the Empire*, p. 85.

for multiple terrorist acts. This Sunni Islamic government in Libya would easily join a confederation to destroy Israel.

Many People

The mention of "many people" in Ezekiel 38 may mean that many other nations or groups will join in the invasion and battle. Yet, it may also mean that each nation specified brought large groups of people and there is a massive invasion of people from these nations.

Interpreters such as Phillip Goodman believe that this phrase implies that the nations immediately surrounding Israel will also be involved in the Magog war against Israel.[80] They think that this inner ring of nations will join the outer ring of nations mentioned in the Bible to attack Israel in the near future. This would include the inner ring of nations mentioned in the last chapter dealing with Psalm 83.

But because the text is not clear, we cannot be certain of what is meant more than a large group of people and massive armies are coming to attack.

Sheba and Dedan

While the Bible lists the invading nations, Ezekiel tells us that several nations will protest the invasion. *"Sheba and Dedan, and the merchants of Tarshish, with all the young lions thereof, shall say unto thee, Art thou come to take a spoil? hast thou gathered thy company to take a prey? to carry away silver and gold, to take away cattle and goods, to take a great spoil?"* (Ezekiel 38:13).

Although some believe that Sheba and Dedan are referring to sections of modern Jordan, it seems that Dr. Hitchcock has again done the best research to discover their identification. He tells us: "Sheba and Dedan are easy to locate. They're the modern nations of Saudi Arabia and

---

80. Philip Goodman, *The Psalm 83 Prophecy*, p. 6.

the more moderate Gulf States. These Sunni Muslims are vehemently opposed to Iran and its nuclear quest."[81]

Sheba was the area where the Queen of Sheba ruled. It was in the area of the modern Gulf states of the Persian Gulf. Dedan was an ancient oasis city and capital of one of Arabia's oldest kingdoms in the northwestern region of the Arabian Peninsula. Today these areas are Yemen and Saudi Arabia.

As the nations of Russia, the additional central Asian nations, Turkey, Iran, Sudan, and Libya prepare to invade, these other nations will protest but choose to not get involved in the conflict. They will send ambassadors to object and complain, but not help with either side of the conflict.

The Merchants of Tarshish

Another nation that brings opposition to the Magog war is called the Merchants of Tarshish. In ancient times, the city of Tarshish was a Phoenician colony on the coast of Spain. This was the city where Jonah was planning to flee (Jonah 1:1–3) when God brought him to the area of Nineveh through a special whale journey to preach repentance to the people.

Jonah had tried to flee as far west as possible to the last area of the known world instead of going east to Nineveh. Tarshish was the farthest known western location in his day. Because this section also mentions "the young lions," it is sometimes interpreted as applying to the furthest Western powers of today.

This has led to the concept that this name applies to Spain and the nations that spawned from her would include Central and South America. Another concept is that it applies to England (also considered Tarshish or the furthest point of the empire in later history).

---

81. Mark Hitchcock, *Showdown with Iran*, p. 62.

Most of Europe has used an eagle as their national symbol, while England is the land of the lion, as is evident on their national flag. Some have viewed the "young lions" to refer to nations that came from England, especially noting a possible reference to the United States of America, Canada, and Australia. These nations would be "young lions" birthed from the much older lion of England.

While this is a tantalizing thought, it seems most reasonable for the Merchants of Tarshish to refer to an area of Europe, such as Spain or England. But whatever nations are meant by Ezekiel, these nations are either too weak or not motivated to help Israel and they only send ambassadors to object to the war.

One interesting concept raised in this study is the absence of Babylon in the war of Gog and Magog. This is especially telling because Ezekiel was living in Babylon when this prophecy was given, yet the ancient nation was not mentioned. This must mean that Babylon will go through a change in her future that will restrict her from joining in the war.

Babylon was the major world power in Ezekiel's day, and this ancient nation is now known as the modern nation of Iraq. Iraq was a major player in terrorism and war in the twentieth century. After the rule and overthrow of Saddam Hussein in Iraq, Iran has risen as the leader of the region and is seen as the major partner of the area with Russia instead of Iraq.

Dr. Ed Hindson has an intriguing thought as to the reason that Babylon was not mentioned. "In light of current events in the Middle East, it is possible that Iraq will either 1) break into fragmented, warring pieces; 2) be taken over by Iran; or 3) become an international zone under the auspices of the United Nations." [82]

---

82. Hindson, LaHaye, *Global Warning: Are We on the Brink of World War III?*, p. 135.

To make it easier to remember the named combatants, here is a chart of the nations:

The Nations of Gog and Magog	
Magog	The former Soviet republics: Kazakhstan, Kirghizia, Uzbekistan, Turkmenistan, Tajikistan, and Ukraine
Rosh	Russia
Meshech	Turkey
Tubal	Turkey
Gomer	Turkey
Beth-Togarmah	Turkey
Persia	Iran
Ethiopia/Cush	Sudan
Libya	Libya
The Protesters to the Magog War	
Sheba	The Gulf states such as Yemen
Dedan	Saudi Arabia
The Merchants of Tarshish	Spain or England

Whatever the case, the nation of Iraq is not mentioned in this war, although she will be a vital part of the world's political power in the Tribulation period to come.

Egypt is another historic enemy of Israel that is not mentioned in the Magog invasion. This list of missing nations also includes Lebanon, Syria, Jordan, and others.

Because they are not specifically mentioned in the text, we must be silent as to their possible involvement in the Magog conflict.

After reviewing the nations involved in the Magog war, there are three views as to the identification of the invading nations and the locations of their movements. This is primarily based on variations as to the identity of Gomer.

In a conservative view, Gomer is the original location of the Cimmerians and so Israel is invaded by Turkey joining with Russia and the other nations. In a moderate view, Gomer is the Eastern European nations joining Russia, as well as Turkey and the other nations. And in a broad view, Gomer is Germany, joined with the Eastern European nations and Russia, as well as all the other allied nations.

Now that we have seen conclusively who is involved in the Magog invasion, we need to look at the details of this coming invasion of Israel from her enemies. The Bible gives us a detailed scenario of the Magog war in Ezekiel 38–39.

CHAPTER EIGHT

THE PLAN OF THE GOG AND MAGOG WAR

By studying the text of Ezekiel 38–39, we can see a great amount of information on this prophesied Magog war. As a result, we will look at who, where, why, what, how, and when this war will happen. We have seen who is involved, and now we will see the other details.

Where Is This Invasion of Israel?

The prophet tells us where the coming Gog and Magog conflict will happen. Ezekiel 38:7–9 says,

> *Be thou prepared, and prepare for thyself, thou, and all thy company that are assembled unto thee, and be thou a guard unto them. After many days thou shalt be visited: in the latter years thou shalt come into the land that is brought again from the sword, and is gathered out of many people, against the mountains of Israel, which had been a waste: but it is brought forth out of the nations, and they shall dwell safely all of them. Thou shalt ascend and come like a storm, thou shalt be like a cloud to cover the land, thou, and all thy bands, and many people with thee.*

We can see that the combined forces will come as a storm cloud covering the land and convene at the mountains of Israel. This means there must be a nation of Israel by the time of the battle. Because of this passage, we know that there must be a Jewish state "in the latter years" or in the end times. Israel must be regathered in unbelief because only in this state of unbelief will many turn to the Lord after the invasion.

The passage also mentions that the armies will be assembled at the mountains of Israel. The nation of Israel has a mountain range running down the middle of the country. These mountains extend the length of the country from the southern point of the Valley of Jezreel at the point of Jenin in Galilee in the north until they diminish north of Beersheba in the Negev in the south. This is where the nations come to fight.

This is a land brought back from the sword (after several years of fighting and persecution). It is a land gathered out of many people (the Jews are regathered from many nations). This is a land with mountains that have been a continual waste (Israel was a desolate place before their return). And Israel is a land brought forth out of the peoples where the nation could dwell in safety.

All of these prerequisites are true of modern Israel. Since the return of the Jewish people especially since 1948, the people of Israel have regathered from places of persecution from numerous nations of the world and rebuilt what was a desolate land into a successful nation. Because of these conditions, the attack is unexpected as if Israel is living in relative peace and security.

Why Does This Invasion of Israel Happen?

Next, Ezekiel tells us *why* this invasion will occur. Ezekiel 38:10–13 says:

> *Thus saith the Lord God; It shall come to pass, that at the same time shall things come into thy mind, and thou shall think an evil thought: And thou shalt say, I will go up to the land of unwalled villages; I will go to them that are at rest, that dwell safely, all of them dwelling without*

walls, and having neither bars nor gates, To take a spoil, and to take a prey; to turn thine hand upon the desolate places that are now inhabited, and upon the people that are gathered out of the nations, which have gotten cattle and goods, that dwell in the midst of the land. Sheba, and Dedan, and the merchants of Tarshish, with all the young lions thereof, shall say unto thee, Art thou come to take a spoil? hast thou gathered thy company to take a prey? to carry away silver and gold, to take away cattle and goods, and to take a great spoil?

The combined armies of Gog come to a land of unwalled villages, living without gates or bars. This prophecy could be a description of modern Israel because the cities and towns are built without protective walls and they are not suspecting this coming huge attack.

The mention of Sheba and the merchants of Tarshish pointing to the underlying purpose of the war is tied to the background of these locations. In ancient times, Sheba was a major source of trade from the area of Saudi Arabia and the Gulf states, and the merchants of Tarshish were involved in trade from Spain and locations in Africa. These merchant nations see the economic reason that the war was undertaken: to loot the country of Israel of her wealth.

The purpose of the invasion is for spoil. The text uses the common Old Testament terms to describe spoil such as *cattle and goods* and *silver and gold*. Other items of spoil have also been suggested as the actual cause of the invasion, such as the Dead Sea quantity of 45 billion tons of sodium, chlorine, sulfur, potassium, calcium, magnesium, and bromide, but Russia could acquire this by invading Jordan as well.

Sometimes it is suggested that Russia comes to take the natural gas of Israel. Fox News reported on March 29,

2013, "Recent discoveries of massive offshore natural gas deposits [for Israel]."[83] National Geographic reported on July 3, 2012, "New Natural Gas Wealth Means Historic Change for Israel."[84] Israel has discovered gas and even oil, but not in the quantities of other regions. However, this is a source of riches. The text does not clearly name the content of the spoil, so we can only know that these nations come for wealth.

Yet, the primary reason seems to be to get the land of Israel. This would give Russia a key foothold in the Middle East and rid the Arabs of their primary enemy, the Jewish people. It seems that the spoil of Israel is only a pretext to get the land. Notice the verses of the Magog conflict in context. Ezekiel 38:10 and 12 says,

> *Thus saith the Lord God; It shall come to pass, that at the same time shall things come into thy mind, and thou*

83. www.foxnews.com/with-natural-gas-discoveries-Israel
84. www.news.nationalgeographic.com/news/energy/2012/07/120793-israel-new-natural-gas/

*shall think an evil thought: ... To take a spoil, and to take a prey; to turn thine hand upon **the desolate places** [the land] that are now inhabited, and upon **the people** that are gathered out of the nations, which have gotten cattle and goods, that dwell in the midst of the land.* [emphasis added]

To show that the real objective is to get the land and destroy the Jewish people, God then tells us in Ezekiel 38:16,

*And thou shalt come up **against my people** of Israel, as a cloud to cover the land; it shall be in the latter days, and I will bring thee **against my land,** that the heathen may know me, when I shall be sanctified in thee, O Gog, before their eyes. [emphasis added]*

Phillip Goodman clarifies the real objective is not the spoil but the land and people of Israel. With astute perception he states, "As wealthy as Israel is, or will ever get, the real goal of the invading Russian-Islamic coalition is to wipe out the people and to take the land."[85]

Then the question of *why* this invasion happens is answered from God's perspective. Ezekiel 38:14–16 says:

Therefore, son of man, prophesy and say unto Gog, Thus saith the LORD God; In that day when my people of Israel dwelleth safely, shalt thou not know of it? And thou shalt come from thy place out of the north parts, thou, and many people with thee, all of them riding upon horses, a great company, and a mighty army: And thou shalt come up against my people of Israel, as a cloud to cover the land; it shall be in the latter days, and I will bring thee against my land, that the heathen may know me, when I shall be sanctified in thee, O Gog, before their eyes.

---

85. Philip Goodman, *The Psalm 83 Prophecy*, p. 2.

Because the vast army of Gog is made up of many nations from different cultures, races, and languages, they will become so confused that the armies will attack and kill each other in the aftermath. This will be a tremendous example of friendly fire, as the attacking nations through confusion unknowingly attack their own allies instead of Israel. Rather than fighting Israel, they will actually attack each other instead.

What Is Involved in This Invasion of Israel?

An interesting review of *what* is involved is next given by Ezekiel. Ezekiel 38:17–18 says:

> *Thus saith the Lord God; Art thou he of whom I have spoken in old time by my servants the prophets of Israel, which prophesied in those days many years that I would bring thee against them? And it shall come to pass at the same time when Gog shall come against the land of Israel, saith the Lord God, that my fury shall come up in my face.*

In these verses, God tells us that His fury is raised because the nations come to attack Israel, His chosen people and the apple of His eye. The war initiates the fury of the Lord. This reminds us that God is always watching over Israel and He knows what is happening in the affairs of men.

How Will This Invasion of Israel Happen?

The prophet tells us *how* this invasion unfolds in Ezekiel 38:19–23:

> *For in my jealousy and in the fire of my wrath have I spoken, Surely in that day there shall be a great shaking in the land of Israel; So that the fishes of the sea, and the*

fowls of the heaven, and the beasts of the field, and all creeping things that creep upon the earth, and all the men that are upon the face of the earth, shall shake at my presence, and the mountains shall be thrown down, and the steep places shall fall, and every wall shall fall to the ground. And I will call for a sword against him throughout all my mountains, saith the Lord GOD; every man's sword shall be against his brother. And I will plead against him with pestilence and with blood; and I will rain upon him, and upon his bands, and upon the many people that are with him, an overflowing rain, and great hailstones, fire, and brimstone. Thus will I magnify myself, and sanctify myself; and I will be known in the eyes of many nations, and they shall know that I am the LORD.

When the combined armies of Gog converge on Israel, no opposing army is mentioned in fighting with Magog's forces. God Himself, by supernatural means, will destroy the invading army. How does God bring this judgment?

1. God Sends a Great Earthquake

As the vast armies come like a sudden storm and cover the land of Israel like a cloud, and as they are getting into position to attack, suddenly a great earthquake occurs that separates the land into deep chasms. Because of the earthquake, the mountains and high places are moved and many of the heights fall, killing part of the army in its wake.

The animals of the world and the creatures of sea life will all feel the movement of God in this earthquake. Many areas of cities and towns will be destroyed as the walls of buildings and retaining walls collapse. One commentator mentioned that he believed that every wall in Israel would collapse. This earthquake is so tremendous in strength that it is felt around the entire world. And this obviously throws the armies into mass confusion.

2. There Is Infighting Between the Troops
When the great earthquake occurs, just as the armies are assembling into place, suddenly there is also great confusion in Gog's forces. They have been concentrating on their attack, and now they have to deal with the moving of the Earth, the falling mountains and hills, the new landscape of the area, and communication difficulties.

Because the vast army of Gog is made up of many nations from different cultures, races, and languages, they will become so confused that the armies will attack and kill each other in the aftermath. This will be a tremendous example of the results of friendly fire, as the attacking nations through confusion unknowingly attack their own allies instead of Israel. They will think they are attacking a defense force from Israel when they will actually attack each other instead.

3. The Coming of Pestilence and Plagues
As a result of the attack, God also sends pestilence, and, unexpectedly, disease and plague break out among the soldiers. These incurable, lethal plagues will inflict and kill many people. This is a common result of war, and this plague could continue and broaden its impact as any surviving soldiers return to their homeland and take it with them to spread the plague to their place of origin. It could also be the result of chemical warfare or biochemical warfare.

4. The Falling of Fire and Brimstone
During the battle, there will come intense, driving rain and then fire and brimstone will fall from the sky, consuming

a mass of the combined army in a fiery blaze of destruction. The intense rains will cause torrents of flooding and hinder their attack.

The hailstones and fire and brimstone are reminiscent of the earlier judgment of Sodom and Gomorrah, cities that were completely destroyed. Because of the earthquake, volcanic activity occurs which brings erupting fire and brimstone, similar to being in the middle of an erupting volcano.

Although it has taken time to gather these various armies and for them to travel to Israel and position themselves to attack, once God steps into the battle in judgment, the destruction of the enemy forces and the conclusion of the battle is quick and decisive. Gog's forces are destroyed and Gog's purpose of evil for Israel is miraculously overthrown.

5. Fiery Destruction on the Enemy Homeland

There is also another unusual element in this conflict. God not only destroys the invading armies, but He also sends fire and brimstone to destroy the military resources of their individual homelands to such a point that none of these nations will be able to raise an additional army to fight.

This collateral damage decimates the invading nations and they are no longer a threat to Israel or any other nation. Even the most powerful nations, such as Russia and Iran, will no longer be a major world military power and all the invading nations will have a crippled and decimated military as a result. Ezekiel 39:6 says: *"And I will send a fire on Magog, and among them that dwell carelessly in the isles: that they shall know that I am the LORD."*

About this verse, Joel Rosenberg tells us:

> This suggests that targets throughout Russia and the

former Soviet Union, as well as Russia's allies, will be supernaturally struck on this day of judgment and partially or completely consumed. These could be limited to nuclear missile silos, military bases, radar installations, defense ministries, intelligence headquarters, and other government buildings of various kinds. But such targets could very well also include religious centers such as mosques, madrassas, Islamic schools and universities, and other facilities that preach hatred against Jews and Christians and call for the destruction of Israel. Either way, we will have to expect extensive collateral damage, and many civilians will be at severe risk.[86]

This fiery destruction in the homeland of enemy nations will be a strong testament that God has brought this judgment and shown them the error of attacking Israel. The purpose of this homeland judgment is to show the people that God is the Lord and the only true God of this world. *The Liberty Bible Commentary* sums up the Magog war events quite well,

The greatest military power in the world will not be able to stand when God lets loose His fury by causing mountains, valleys, and buildings to be leveled. Added to this will be inundating floods, fire, and brimstone through volcanic eruptions, and even confusion in the troops taking each other's lives, perhaps as an escape from the holocaust of the elements. Thus, God will be magnified, because it will be recognized that the Lord has done this.[87]

---

86. Joel C. Rosenberg, *Epicenter: Why the Current Rumblings in the Middle East Will Change Your Future* (Carol Stream, IL: Tyndale, 2000), 165.

87. Ed Hindson, gen. ed., Elmer Janz, "Ezekiel." *The Liberty Bible Commentary—Old Testament* (Nashville, TN: Thomas Nelson, 1982), 1605.

The Aftermath of the Magog War

Using the Law of Recurrence, where God sometimes repeats a prophecy and gives more detail, God tells us more details of the war and its aftermath in Ezekiel 39. Ezekiel 39:1–5 says:

> *Therefore, thou son of man, prophesy against Gog, and say, Thus saith the Lord God; Behold, I am against thee, O Gog, the chief prince of Meshech and Tubal: And I will turn thee back, and leave but the sixth part of thee, and will cause thee to come up from the north parts, and will bring thee upon the mountains of Israel: And I will smite thy bow out of thy left hand, and will cause thine arrows to fall out of thy right hand. Thou shalt fall upon the mountains of Israel, thou, and all thy bands, and the people that is with thee: I will give thee unto the ravenous birds of every sort, and to the beasts of the field to be devoured. Thou shalt fall upon the open field: for I have spoken it, saith the Lord God.*

Although the Authorized Version says that one-sixth of the army of Gog survives, other commentators believe that this verse actually means there will be total destruction of Gog's invading forces. Whatever the case, the army was originally described as so huge that it looked like a cloud coming to cover the land of Israel and the destruction of the forces will be so large that it will take an entire valley to bury the dead. By the end of the conflict, at least five-sixths of the combined invading armies or possibly more will be killed during this war and it will be a complete defeat of the enemies of Israel.

While the nations have gathered in the mountains of Israel to fight, God attacks them and disables their ability to attack Israel. This action is described as being similar to

God knocking the weapons out of their hands (verse 3). Then the invading forces of multiple nations will be destroyed as they gather on the mountains and open fields to attack.

The Knowledge of God Will Come to Israel

Ezekiel 39:7 says: *"So will I make my holy name known in the midst of my people Israel; and I will not let them pollute my holy name any more: and the heathen shall know that I am the LORD, the Holy One in Israel."*

As a result of this war, this invasion will be a testament to the supernatural working of God on behalf of Israel. Because the invading forces are decimated and destroyed through supernatural means by the power of God, it will be evident that God has brought Israel the victory.

This will not be a war won through the fighting of the Israeli Defense Forces or assisted by America or any other country. This war is not won by any conventional warfare. As far as it is known, not even a shot is fired in defense of Israel. It is clearly a rescue of Israel by God.

This will cause many of the Jewish people to see and understand the supernatural working of God and they will believe in the Lord. In the Bible, the Jewish people always require a sign to see that God is working. This will be a clear sign to the Jewish people that God has moved supernaturally to save His people and that He cares for the Jewish nation.

God's name will not only be sanctified among the Gentile nations but His name will be sanctified among the Jews of Israel as well. This action will point people to God and many Jews will begin to know the Lord and return to Him as there is a great revival among the Jewish people.

Also, this is probably one of the main factors to bring about the 144,000 believing Jewish witnesses of the Tribulation period. The Bible tells us that He will additionally send an angel to proclaim the Gospel, and two witnesses will arise to preach for the first three and a half years.

As a result, 144,000 Jewish witnesses, 12,000 from each tribe, will witness the Gospel to the world during this Tribulation period. The saving of the nation of Israel during the Magog war could be the first step in bringing the nation back to know the Lord and this could be the catalyst to begin the spiritual awakening of the 144,000 Jews to come to know God.

The Grand Finale of the Magog War

Because so many people are killed and there is such widespread death of the army and an abundance of leftover weapons, a cleanup of the war is begun and continues for seven years. Ezekiel 39:9–16 says,

> *And they that dwell in the cities of Israel shall go forth, and shall set on fire and burn the weapons, both the shields and the bucklers, the bows and the arrows, and the handstaves, and the spears, and they shall burn them with fire seven years: So that they shall take no wood out of the field, neither cut down any out of the forests; for they shall burn the weapons with fire: and they shall spoil those that spoiled them, and rob those that robbed them, saith the Lord GOD. And it shall come to pass in that day, that I will give unto Gog a place there of graves in Israel, the valley of the passengers on the east of the sea: and it shall stop the noses of the passengers: and there shall they bury Gog and all his multitude: and they shall call it The valley of Hamongog. And seven months shall the house of Israel be burying of them, that they may cleanse the land. Yea, all the people of the land shall bury them, and it shall be to them a renown the day that I shall be glorified, saith the Lord GOD. And they shall sever*

out men of continual employment, passing through the land to bury with the passengers those that remain upon the face of the earth, to cleanse it: after the end of seven months shall they search. And the passengers that pass through the land, when any man seeth a man's bone, then shall he set a sign by it, till the buriers have buried it in the valley of Hamongog And the name of the city shall be Hamonah. Thus shall they cleanse the land.

The Burying of the Dead

Because the slaughter of the armies is so great with a tremendous loss of life, the Jewish people will spend seven months gathering and burying the dead. This loss of life will be so staggering as to require an entire valley to bury the dead. A new city in the burial valley will arise just to handle the organization, housing, and logistics of the people as they work for seven months to bury the dead. The name of the valley is Hamon-gog which means *Gog's hordes* and the city of Hamonah means *horde*.

The entire nation of Israel will evidently be involved in the search for the dead. Men are hired in full-time employment to search for the bodies while others handle the burying. Even after seven months, it is also commonplace for anyone traveling throughout the land to continue to find bodies and bones of the dead, to have a specified way to mark the location of the dead and alert the authorities, and for these bones to be transported to the valley of burying.

Dr. Hitchcock brilliantly sums up the results of this Magog war and the resulting death, "These nations will arrogantly, boldly swoop down on Israel to take her land, but the only piece of land they will claim in Israel is their burial plots (Ezekiel 39:12). They will set out to bury Israel, but God will bury them."[88]

---
88. Mark Hitchcock, *Iran: The Coming Crises* (Sisters, OR: Multnomah, 2006), p. 172.

The Burning of the Weapons

There is also a gathering of the weapons of the decimated invading armies. The text tells us that so many weapons are found that the weapons are burned for seven years. There is no need to cut down trees for fuel for fire because the people will burn the weapons during an entire seven-year period.

This has led to several questions. In our modern world, why would nations come to attack with horses and weapons that were also used in ancient times such as bows, arrows, spears, and shields? Modern weapons including guns and tanks are usually made of metal such as steel, which would not burn like wooden weapons. So, why are more primitive weapons mentioned?

Weapons of bows and arrows are noted in Ezekiel 39:3. While these weapons were common at the time of Ezekiel, they have been used throughout history, such as in historical battles in England and Europe. Bows and arrows were also in the Vietnam War because it is a silent weapon and the enemy may not know how to determine the source of fire. Yet some scholars believe this passage means modern weapons which could also take even years to destroy.

Recently, research has begun the use of an alternate form of weapon. Instead of using metal, which can be scanned using radar and modern heat-seeking scanners, they have tried to build weapons and equip transport vehicles using lignostone, a type of wood component.

Lignostone is used in cryogenic operations, as a special type of wood for transformers, and can be used as the main component of switchboards. It has low thermal conductivity, low and high temperature resistance, and it is highly resistant to abrasion and wear. This concept was first used by the British to build bridges and now it is possibly being utilized by the Russians to build weapons.

If the weapons and transport vehicles utilized this material for their structure and bodywork, and they were able to make rifles and trucks from this material, then it would be impervious to radar and heat scanning. Also, when captured, these weapons and vehicles would burn like wood. This could be the modern answer as to how the weapons, ancient or modern, would actually burn.[89]

Dr. John Walvoord has a summary of this question: "No final answer can be given why primitive weapons are specified. Though the outcome of the battle was clearly prophesied, Scripture does not offer any explanation why the weapons described are primitive."[90]

Whatever the case, the weapons used in this Magog invasion are burned for seven years and used as fuel.

The Call for a Feast for Wildlife

God calls for the birds and animals to come to a feast and to partake of the dead. Ezekiel 39:17–20 says,

> *And, thou son of man, thus saith the Lord God; Speak unto every feathered fowl, and to every beast of the field, Assemble yourselves, and come; gather yourselves on every side to my sacrifice that I do sacrifice for you, even a great sacrifice upon the mountains of Israel that ye may eat flesh, and drink blood. Ye shall eat the flesh of the mighty, and drink the blood of the princes of the earth, of rams, and lambs, and of goats, of bullocks, all of them fatlings of Bashan. And ye shall eat fat till ye be full, and drink blood till ye be drunken, of my sacrifice which I have sacrificed for you. Thus shall ye be filled at my table with horses and chariots, with mighty men, and with all men of war, saith the Lord God.*

---

89. "Ezekiel 38/39…Weapons of War," Accessed on Aug. 25, 2024, https://tapatalk.com
90. John F. Walvoord, *Every Prophecy of the Bible,* p. 196.

Because the number of people in the army is so vast with so many invading soldiers, the birds of the air and beasts of the field come to dine on the carnage. This slaughter will include the people, their horses, and even mighty men and men of war. In other words, all the people both great and small (or the common soldiers and their important leaders) will die and be left to be eaten by birds and animals until they can finally be buried in the specified valley.

God Restores the Nation of Israel

Ezekiel 39:21–29 says:

And I will set my glory among the heathen, and all the heathen shall see my judgment that I have executed, and my hand that I have laid upon them. So the house of Israel shall know that I am the LORD their God from that day and forward. And the heathen shall know that the house of Israel went into captivity for their iniquity: because they trespassed against me, therefore hid I my face from them, and gave them into the hand of their enemies: so fell they all by the sword. According to their uncleanness and according to their transgressions have I done unto them, and hid my face from them. Therefore thus saith the Lord GOD; Now will I bring again the captivity of Jacob, and have mercy upon the whole house of Israel, and will be jealous for my holy name; After that they have borne their shame, and all their trespasses whereby they have trespassed against me, when they dwelt safely in their land, and none made them afraid. When I have brought them again from the people, and gathered them out of their enemies' lands, and am sanctified in them in the sight of many nations; Then shall they know that I am the LORD their God, which caused them to be led into captivity among the heathen: but I have gathered them unto their own land,

and have left none of them any more there. Neither will I hide my face any more from them: for I have poured out my spirit upon the house of Israel, saith the Lord God.

God reiterates and explains how He has come to save Israel and some of the Jewish people turn to the Lord. In this passage, God tells how He will restore the Jewish people to their land and they will return to God. Just as they were taken into captivity in the time of Ezekiel because of their iniquity, God will have mercy on His people and regather them back to their own land.

We know from other verses that this regathering happens gradually over several years leading up to and during the Tribulation period. God has been regathering the Jewish people back to Israel, especially since 1948 and their declaration of statehood. And some Jewish people will believe in God as a result of the Magog war. But the final spiritual return of the Jewish people will happen at the end of the Campaign of Armageddon.

The climatic event mentioned in this passage is that God's Spirit returns to the house of Jacob. God will have a people that have experienced the New Covenant of Jeremiah 49. This means that they will return to the Lord, believe on Him, and have His Spirit in their heart. One day, the entire nation of Israel will believe on the Lord.

When Is This Invasion of Israel to Occur?

Perhaps the most controversial question of the Magog invasion is the timing of *when* this war is to occur. There are multiple theories and we will deal with the primary possibilities.

Because the text tells us that this war occurs "in the latter years" (Ezekiel 38:8) and "in the latter days" (Ezekiel 38:16), this war is obviously future and has a last-day fulfillment. *The Liberty Bible Commentary* states, "The phrase *After many days* and *in the latter years* very clearly projects the events to the distant future of Israel's last days before the Second Coming."[91]

The question remains: When in the last days does this Magog war occur? There are at least five possibilities for future fulfillment. Because this author takes the position that this war will occur before the Tribulation, we will look at that view last. Let us examine the possibilities of each of the views.

In the First Part of the Tribulation

A very popular view is that the Magog war will occur during the Tribulation period near to the end of the first half. This view is held because the phrase *dwelling securely* is thought to refer to a peace that results from Israel's covenant with the Antichrist (Dan. 9:27). Also, this invasion is thought to be the same as the invasion of the "king of the north" in Daniel 11:40.

However, to dwell securely does not necessarily mean to dwell in peace, but rather it could be to dwell in confidence against any unknown foe. About the timing happening in the middle of Tribulation, Dr. Fruchtenbaum notes: "It is hard to see why God would intervene at this point on Israel's behalf and then immediately allow the events of the second half of the Tribulation Period to commence, doing a great amount of damage to Israel."[92]

While we agree that the Daniel 11 events happen in the middle of the Tribulation, the king of the north in Daniel 11 is not Gog of Ezekiel 38–39. The context of Daniel 11 repeatedly refers to the king of the north as the king of Syria and the king of the south as the king of Egypt.

Interpreters who hold this view try to inconsistently

---

91. Ed Hindson, gen. ed., Elmer Janz, "Ezekiel." *The Liberty Bible Commentary—Old Testament,* p. 1604.

92. Fruchtenbaum, *The Footsteps of Messiah,* pp. 77–78.

make the mention of this king of the north in verse 40 refer to Russia while the other verses would be seen as the king of Syria, but consistent contextual interpretation would make this mention also be the king of Syria. This means that the invasion of Daniel 11:40 is distinct from the invasion in Ezekiel 38-39.

There is also the mention of burying the dead for seven months and burning the weapons for seven years. Because there is a cleansing of the land after the Campaign of Armageddon, the burning of the weapons must also be finished before the Millennium, and this seven-year burning could not be finished in three and a half years.

And while the Jews are escaping from Antichrist, they would not be able to stop to search for bodies, bury the dead, and build a new city while they are under persecution and fleeing for their lives. Thus, the Magog war could not happen during the seven-year Tribulation.

During the Campaign of Armageddon

Another view is that the Magog war happens at the end of the Tribulation together with the Campaign of Armageddon. While the Campaign of Armageddon does happen at the end of the Tribulation, this will not include the Magog war.

There are distinctions between the two wars. The Magog war mentions only certain allies that join them in the conflict, and other nations are mentioned that object to Magog's war. Yet in Armageddon, all nations are involved in the invasion of Israel and there are no objecting nations. In the Magog war, they come to attack Israel in the mountains of Israel, while in Armageddon, the nations assemble in the Valley of Armageddon.

In the Ezekiel conflict, they come to Israel from the north, while in Armageddon, the nations come from the whole Earth. The purpose of the Magog invasion is to take spoil while the purpose of Armageddon is to kill all of the Jews. The Magog invasion is destroyed through the convolutions of nature while the Armageddon invaders are destroyed by the appearance of Christ and His spoken Word.

The Ezekiel invaders are destroyed on the mountains of Israel while the Armageddon invaders are destroyed between Petra and Jerusalem. And the Magog invasion occurs as Israel is living securely while Armageddon happens as Israel is in flight and hiding.[93]

In the Beginning of the Millennium

Sometimes, it is suggested that this Magog invasion occurs between the Tribulation and the Millennium. While the Bible mentions an interlude of seventy-five days between Armageddon and the Millennium (Dan, 12:12), this is because the Temple's desecration will last thirty days beyond the Tribulation and there are also forty-five days for other events.

Daniel 12:7 tells us the latter half of the Tribulation will be 1,260 days long (or three and a half years) while Daniel 12:11 tells us the Temple desecration is 1,290 days, which is thirty days longer. There is a special blessing for those who live to 1,335 days after this time (Dan. 12:12), which must mean that those who were not killed will enter the Millennium.

Yet, there is not time for all the Ezekiel events of the Magog war and aftermath to happen in only seventy-five days. This would include the time to invade, the war itself, the burial of the dead for seven months, and the burning of the weapons for seven years, which cannot happen in seventy-five days.

---

93. Ibid., pp. 78–79.

At the End of the Millennium

An additional view is that the Ezekiel 38-39 war is the same as the Magog final rebellion of Revelation 20:7-9. Because both events mention Gog and Magog, it is assumed that these events are the same. But the names could also be used in a general way to show the concept of people coming to attack Israel and not mean the same event.

In the Ezekiel invasion, the people come from the north, while in Revelation 20, they come from the whole world. And there is again the problem of burying the dead for seven months and burning the weapons for seven years.

The Ezekiel invasion is an armed combination of certain nations that come to attack, they are destroyed, buried, and their weapons burned over a seven-year time. The Revelation 20 Gog and Magog rebellion is a quick destruction of the people by fire from Heaven, and it is immediately followed by the dissolution of the Earth (when the Earth is destroyed by fire), and by the Great White Throne Judgment, and the New Heaven and New Earth.

There is simply no time for the burying of the dead and burning of the weapons without this happening during the eternal New Heaven and New Earth which is not possible, so the Ezekiel invasion must be a different event at an earlier time.

Before the Tribulation

There is also the view that the Magog war happens before the Tribulation actually begins, and this is the view of this author. This view holds that Israel is returned to the land, the nation is reestablished and living securely in the land, a Russian coalition invades Israel during her security, and they are supernaturally destroyed by the Lord.

Today, Israel is a land brought back from the sword (from many years of persecution and wars), she is regathered from many nations, the waste places are restored, and she is secured (Ezekiel 38:8–11). While Israel is living securely, this phrase is sometimes taken to mean living at peace. But what is the meaning of living securely? Dr. Fruchtenbaum tells us:

> They dwell securely (Ezek. 38:11, 14). This is sometimes misconstrued as meaning a state of peace. But this is not the meaning of the Hebrew word *batach*. The nominal form of this root means "security." This is not the security due to a state of peace, but a security due to confidence in their own strength. This, too, is a good description of Israel today.
>
> Today, Israel is secure, confident that their army can repel any invasion from the Arab states. Hence, Israel is dwelling securely. Israel is dwelling in unwalled villages (Ezek. 38:11). This is a very good description of the present-day kibbutzim in Israel.[94]

Today, Russia is a major world power that could lead the invasion, and this view gives time to have the Magog war and to bury the dead and burn the weapons before the time of the Millennium. All other views have problems with the seven-month burial and seven-year burning of the weapons.

While this Ezekiel war comes in Ezekiel 38–39, this view is sometimes objected to because it comes during the restoration of Israel. But this Magog invasion comes during the restoration of Israel in unbelief and the restoration of Israel in belief and full faith as a unified nation comes in Ezekiel 40–48. So, the Magog war happens while she is still in unbelief.

One objection is that this view would not agree with the doctrine of the imminency of the Coming of Christ. Some

---

94. Ibid., p. 80.

people believe this pre-Tribulation view would mean that there is an event such as this Magog war that must precede the Rapture. But the Bible does not mention any event that precedes the Rapture.

The Bible tells us that the Second Coming of Jesus involves several events. In the first part of His coming, Jesus returns to take the believers to Heaven. This event is described in 1 Thessalonians 4:13–18. In verses 16 and 17, the Bible says, *"For the Lord himself shall descend from heaven with a shout, with the voice of the archangel, and with the trump of God: and the dead in Christ shall rise first: Then we which are alive and remain shall be caught up together with them in the clouds, to meet the Lord in the air: and so shall we ever be with the Lord."*

In this passage, all believers from the Church Age on Earth with be taken to Heaven. The bodies of the dead in Christ (the Christian believers) shall be raised and changed into a glorified and resurrected body, and all living believers will be caught up (or raptured) to meet the Lord in the air to then go to Heaven.

The Bible tells us that Jesus could return at any moment and no man knows the day or the hour (Matt. 24:36). This author believes that this verse includes the lack of knowledge of the year, the season, the month, or any detail that might designate Jesus' return in the Rapture for believers. Jesus could come at any moment, so *"be ye also ready: for in such an hour as ye think not the Son of man cometh"* (Matt. 24:44).

The Magog war could come before or after the Rapture. The Rapture is not the event that begins the Tribulation, but the Tribulation starts at the signing of a peace covenant with Israel by the Antichrist (Dan. 9:27).

While this Magog invasion could occur before the Rapture, it is not a sign of the Rapture, and its occurrence before or after the Rapture does not hinder the imminent coming of Jesus at the Rapture. Thus, the Magog invasion could happen before the Tribulation. It is more likely to happen between the Rapture and the Tribulation.

Another objection is that the nation of Israel would return to the Lord after the Magog war, and then how could she apostatize so quickly afterward? Yet, Israel often would turn to the Lord and then apostatize in her history. And the context in Ezekiel 38 does not tell us that the entire nation turns to God, so this could still be the beginning of the return of the nation to God, such as the coming of the 144,000 Jews to faith in God.

Sometimes, the latter days timing is taken to mean that it is pre-Rapture. But the phrase *latter days* applies to the entire period of the end times including the end of the Church Age as well as the coming of the Tribulation, thus the war can easily be pre-Tribulational.

Could Israel soon experience this terrible invasion? Israel is back in her land and the war could happen at any time before the Tribulation. To see this timing in more detail, let us examine: What are the events that will happen before the Tribulation?

The Order of Events Before the Tribulation

For the prophetic future as the Day of the Lord approaches, the Bible warns about a destined time of difficulty for Israel called the "time of Jacob's trouble." She will again make an alliance for false peace, trusting in herself instead of God. This false peace is at the beginning of the Tribulation period and is described as a sudden birth pain (1 Thessalonians 5:3). Just as a mother goes through a series of birth pains before giving birth to a child, the world will go through several birth pains before the coming of the new age and Kingdom.

The Bible mentions nine birth pains that lead to the coming of the Tribulation period:

1. The Beginning of world wars (2 Chron. 15:1–7; Matt. 24: 7–8)
2. The re-establishment of Israel (Ezek. 36: 22–24)
3. Jerusalem will be under Jewish control (Dan. 9:27; Rev. 11:1–2)
4. The Russian invasion of Israel will occur (Ezek. 38:1–39:16)
5. The one-world government will form (Dan. 7:23–24)
6. The ten nations will emerge (Dan. 7:24)
7. Antichrist will rise to power (Dan. 7:24; 2 Thess. 2:1–3)
8. There will be a period of peace and false security (1 Thess. 5:1–3)
9. Antichrist will confirm a seven-year peace covenant with Israel (Dan. 9:27)

Although we must take care to not espouse "newspaper exegesis" (interpreting Bible prophecy from current events), we can easily see that current trends in Israel do match some of these coming events.

We have seen the beginning of world wars with the occurrence of World War I and World War II. Israel was reestablished as a nation and declared her statehood on March 14, 1948. And Jerusalem was recaptured and is under Jewish control as a result of the Six-Day War of 1967.

Israel's future invasion by Russia and a northeastern confederation of nations that are primarily Islamic does seem to be a more realistic possibility today. Russia is economically depressed; she could use Israel's resources and warm seaport and she will be pulled into the conflict against internal resistance. The Islamic influences upon Russia could easily push her to invade Israel through the lure of their oil and gas resources or through other factors.

Also, the short time of peace and safety is followed by the sudden destruction of the Tribulation period. This would clearly imply that there must be great unrest beforehand for realistic peace and safety to appear to begin in the Middle East. After a long and valiant struggle, Israel will finally feel that she has true peace in her hand and then sudden destruction will come.

Finally, the Antichrist will confirm a peace covenant with Israel, virtually guaranteeing complete serenity through his earthly power. This again indicates continued unrest in the Middle Eastern region until his revealing as Earth's most evil world leader.

Through great diplomacy and genius, he will appear to ultimately solve the Middle Eastern peace issue. This is also thought to be a more realistic possibility because after the destruction of many of Israel's Arab antagonist armies, and the weakening of Russia and other nations because of the Magog war, the Antichrist would be able to more easily guarantee peace in the land of Israel. This is because all of her enemies would be too weak to ever oppose her again.

Thus, the Magog invasion is seen to happen after the rise of world wars, the establishment of Israel, and the gaining of Jerusalem under Jewish control. At any moment, Jesus could return in the Rapture to take believers to Heaven. Then in the situation of current Israel, there would occur the Russian invasion of Ezekiel 39–39 and the other events until the signing of a peace covenant between Israel and the Antichrist. Next will come the dreaded Tribulation period and the seven-year rule by the Antichrist.

CHAPTER NINE

WORLD WAR I OF THE TRIBULATION

After the Rapture of believers, there will be a short interval of unspecified time and several events will occur. These will be the additional birth pains mentioned in the Old Testament. While world wars, the re-establishment of Israel, and the city of Jerusalem coming into Jewish hands have already happened in history, the next birth pains will follow in order. We are now living in the time between the third and fourth birth pains awaiting the Rapture, which could happen at any moment. Immediately after the Rapture will occur the next six birth pains.

These will be the Magog war (Ezek. 38:1–39:16), the one-world government will form (Dan. 7:23–24), the ten nations will emerge (Dan. 7:24), Antichrist will rise to power (Dan. 7:24; 2 Thess. 2:1–3), there will be a period of peace and false security (1 Thess. 5:1–3), and Antichrist will confirm a seven-year peace covenant with Israel (Dan. 9:27).

While it seems that these events would take a long time, when we review the time of the first Gulf War under the earlier American President Bush, this war happened in a very short period of time. Also, when we review the exit of the former Soviet nations from Russia, this occurred rather quickly too. So, it is this author's view that the remaining birth pain events will happen very quickly after the Rapture but the length of time is not specified.

At the end of these events, when the Antichrist confirms a peace covenant with Israel, the Tribulation period will begin.

Extensive details of this Tribulation period are given

in Zephaniah, Isaiah 14, and Revelation 6–19, and they are mentioned in other places. Jeremiah called it "the time of Jacob's trouble" (Jer. 30:7) while Daniel referred to it as "a time of trouble" and as the worst time of all of Israel's history.

Daniel 12:1 says: *"And at that time shall Michael stand up, the great prince which standeth for the children of thy people: and there shall be a time of trouble, such as never was since there was a nation even to that same time: and at that time thy people shall be delivered, every one that shall be found written in the book."*

This will be the time of the greatest difficulty for the Jewish people of all their existence as a nation. That is why in the Bible it is called the time of Jacob's trouble, or Israel's trouble.

Revelation 3:10 gives us another insight into this time: *"Because thou hast kept the word of my patience, I also will keep thee from the hour of temptation [or trial], which shall come upon all the world, to try them that dwell upon the earth."*

Here, the Apostle John tells us that this will be the greatest and most intense time of trial for all the history of the world. That means it will be the worst, most difficult time of all man's existence on Earth and this time of supreme difficulty will cover the entire world.

The Length of the Tribulation

The Tribulation will last exactly seven years. To be more technical, the time will be seven years of three hundred sixty days, or lunar years. This is divided into two sections of three and a half years, and each of these three and a half years has twelve hundred sixty days (Dan. 12).

On the day the Antichrist confirms the covenant with Israel, the Tribulation will begin and it will continue until exactly seven years of three hundred sixty days have passed. Each half is twelve hundred sixty days and it has a total of twenty-five hundred twenty days or seven years.

The first three and a half years are referred to as the first half of the Tribulation period. The second half is referred to as the Great Tribulation because the second half of the seven years will be more intensified judgment and tribulation concluded by the Campaign of Armageddon. Interestingly, the entire Tribulation is two time periods of exactly three and a half years or seven years long, precisely fulfilling the seventh week of Daniel's prophecy (Dan. 9:27).

Earlier, Daniel had explained about the judgment time for Israel of seventy weeks of years in Daniel 9:1–27. Here, he tells us that Israel was taken into captivity for their iniquity and served seventy years in Babylon, but the total number of judgment years would be four hundred ninety years.

They had been previously judged for four hundred eighty-three years which led to the death of Messiah and they are awaiting this final week of seven years of judgment. The final week of years will occur at the end of the age, just before the return of Messiah (Dan. 9:24–27). That is why there is a future seven-year week of judgment for Israel and the world.

The Opening Scene of the Tribulation

In Revelation 6–19, the details of the Tribulation are given as the Seven Seals, the Seven Trumpets, the Mid-Tribulation events, the Seven Bowls of Wrath, and the events of Armageddon and afterward.

In the opening scene of Revelation 4, an angel brings forth a seven-sealed book, which in ancient times was a scroll. This scroll was sealed seven times and no one was able to open the book and know what God had written.

Then appeared the Lion of the tribe of Judah, the Root

of David, the Lamb slain from the foundation of the world. This was the appearance of the glorified Jesus Christ, the Son of God, who is the royal son of Judah, from the prophesied line of David as the Root of David, and the sacrificial Lamb of God who gave Himself for the sins of the world. Thus, the Lord Jesus was deemed worthy to open the book.

The angels praised Jesus, and then the twenty-four elders, who are church pastors now in Heaven, joined in the jubilant time of praise and worship. The term *elder* has always referred in the Bible to a pastor of a church. Hence, the twenty-four elders must be pastors who have gone to Heaven and are representatives of the church in Heaven at this point.

Thus, this event happens after the Church Age. This implies that the Rapture of believers during the Church Age happens before this time by inference.

The four beasts of Heaven, each a picture of the glorified Jesus, then sang a song with the twenty-four church elders and all the assembled millions of angels of Heaven, singing, *"Worthy is the lamb that was slain to receive power, and riches, and wisdom, and strength, and honour, and glory, and blessing"* (Rev. 5:12).

As Jesus unrolled the scroll, He would come to a sealed portion of the scroll. When He broke the seal and read that section, a judgment would come on the world.

After he read the first judgment, he would unroll another part of the scroll, open the seal, and read the next judgment until all seven seals were broken, the judgments read and each judgment was brought to fruition. Then started the seven trumpet judgments, the mid-Tribulation events, the seven bowl judgments, and the last events at Armageddon.

When Jesus opened the first seals of the scroll, there came the four horsemen of the apocalypse. Apocalypse means, "the final destruction of the world." So, these four horsemen are the introduction to Earth's most dramatic and extreme judgment of all time as they open the Tribulation time of judgment.

Revelation 6:1-8 gives us the scene:

And I saw when the Lamb opened one of the seals, and I heard, as it were the noise of thunder, one of the four beasts saying, Come and see. And I saw, and behold a white horse: and he that sat on him had a bow; and a crown was given unto him: and he went forth conquering and to conquer. And when he had opened the second seal, I heard the second beast say, Come and see. And there went out another horse that was red: and power was given to him that sat thereon to take peace from the earth, and that they should kill one another: and there was given unto him a great sword. And when he had opened the third seal, I heard the third beast say, Come and see. And I beheld, and lo a black horse; and he that sat on him had a pair of balances in his hand. And I heard a voice in the midst of the four beasts say, A measure of wheat for a penny, and three measure of barley for a penny; and see thou hurt not the oil and the wine. And when he had opened the fourth seal, I heard the voice of the fourth beast say, Come and see. And I looked, and behold a pale horse: and his name that sat on him was Death, and Hell followed with him. And power was given unto them over the fourth part of the earth, to kill with a sword, and with hunger, and with death, and with the beasts of the earth.

The White Horse Judgment

In this passage of Revelation 6:1-8, the four horsemen each picture future judgments of God. The first seal is the rider on the white horse who had a bow and no arrows. He was given a crown and went forth to conquer nations (Rev. 6:1-2).

This white horse pictures a person of high rank who has a crown. Sometimes, this person has been mistaken to be Jesus Christ, but the Lord Jesus will later wear a *diadem* crown or multiple crowns, as King of Kings and Lord of Lords. And He will be the supreme ruler of the millennial world.

This white horse rider of Revelation 6 wears a little crown called a *stephanos* crown of a victor. This is the first future appearance to the world of the person later known to be the Antichrist, for he will conquer nations and kingdoms until he is the ruler of the one-world government of the Tribulation.

Antichrist is called the "little horn" in Daniel 7:8 because he is first seen as a small leader until he gains popularity, power, and strength and rises to world domination. Antichrist will rise to power, probably from Europe, and will take the attention of the world.

The Antichrist will be the greatest political and military leader ever known. He will possess a powerful intellect, a magnetic personality and will have a meteoric rise to power and prominence. Many people will wonder after him, meaning he will amaze the masses and they will admire him. He will begin his rise as a dynamic and visionary leader who will seem to have boundless solutions to the problems of the world. And the world will be drawn to his leadership.

Yet, later his true nature as an evil leader will be manifest. That is why he is always referred to as the "Beast" of Revelation because in his true nature, he is like an animal and does not have any redeeming qualities of good or compassion but is totally selfish, heartless, cruel, and evil.

The Antichrist is Satan possessed and he will work to destroy all religions, especially Christianity, he will kill believers by the millions, and he will eventually establish a new religion to call all the world to worship himself as a god. He stands against the true God of the Bible and Jesus as the Messiah and Savior of the world. This is why he is often called the Antichrist.

In his early years, he will seem to be a wonderful, god-like ruler who people will be drawn to and so he is seen to be, in some ways, like or similar to Christ. Yet later, when his evil nature is revealed, he will be known to be against Christ, the truth of the Bible and all righteousness, and to be the embodiment of evil. He will then be known as the opposite of Christ and will be Antichrist in all of his being.

Daniel tells us that he is energized by Satan and has great power but he does not do powerful things through his own strength. Mighty works are done "but not by his own power" (Dan. 8:24). His coming will be "after the working of Satan with all power and signs and lying wonders" (2 Thess. 2:9) and Satan will give him his power and authority (Rev. 13:2).

This Antichrist will come as a world leader proclaiming peace to the world. That is why the white horse rider has a bow with no arrows. He is not coming fully armed with weapons, but appears to be powerless, proclaiming peace. But then he begins to conquer nation after nation and becomes a king or a political leader.

The Antichrist will rise through diplomacy and deceit. He will be shrewd and skillful in intrigue, "understanding dark sentences" (Dan. 8:23–25). But he will also use military means to accomplish his purpose. He will destroy to an astonishing degree (he will "destroy wonderfully"). He will also destroy mighty men and the holy people and destroy while they are at ease (Dan. 8:24–25).

This means that he will move to take countries through diplomatic cunning and deceit, and then launch a military campaign that will result in him possessing authority over every tribe and people and tongue and nation (Rev. 13:7).

Dr. David Reagan remarks:

> These verses in Daniel 8:23–25 make it very clear that the Antichrist is going to use both diplomacy and military power to gain control of the world. The likeliest scenario is that he will initially rise to power in Europe through the use of shrewd diplomacy. But he will extend his power from his European base through war.[95]

The Red Horse Judgment

In the second seal judgment of Revelation 6:3–4, we have the coming of a red horse. The rider of this horse takes peace from the world and replaces it with a sword, causing the people of the world to kill each other. This is the coming of war, but this is not just any war. This is the coming of the first war of the Tribulation which is actually World War I of the Tribulation.

In this war, the Antichrist goes forth to conquer, initiating his military conquest of the world. He leads his armies to attack key countries and gradually assumes great power and success. He will have already moved to negotiate for control of nations, but this war will be fought for a duration of much of the first three and a half years as he uses military might to rule the world. Obviously, much death and destruction will result as he moves to accomplish his will and untold numbers of people will die during this war.

He will blaspheme God (Rev. 13:5), make tremendous boasts about himself (Dan. 7:8), and change the calendar and the money system of the world. He will be extremely strong-willed, blasphemous, and full of evil. He will have an empire that will cover the world with the most demonic rule in all history.

---

95. David R. Reagan, *9 Wars of the End Times*, pp. 59–60.

This will be a war when Antichrist sets out to conquer the world by military fighting and destruction and it will encompass the seven seals and seven trumpet judgments of Revelation and endure for three and a half years.

The Black Horse Judgment

The third seal in Revelation 6:5-6 is the black horse whose rider holds the judgment balances in his hand. This judgment will be a time of severe famine for people around the world when hunger and suffering grip the entire Earth. That is why there is the mention of the price of wheat and barley.

Wheat was the normal crop for making bread, and barley was a cheaper type of meal. It was mentioned to show that people will bargain to get even the least expensive food of their day. Oil and wine were examples of food for the wealthy, and this shows that even the wealthy will have problems with hunger and famine.

Famine and death are the results of fighting and war, and this is only one of the sources of death for the people living during this period.

The Pale Horse Judgment

The fourth seal judgment in Revelation 6:7-8 is the rider on the pale horse. This judgment includes four causes of death. This judgment continues death by the sword, meaning death coming through fighting and World War I of the Tribulation. Death will also come from hunger as the famine continues to grow and engulf much of the world.

There will also be death through pestilence, disease, and plagues which will rise quickly through problems caused by this war of Antichrist. Then, ultimately, as so many millions of people are killed, cities are decimated, and people are dying from hunger, disease, and injured or killed through the war, the wild animals will come to attack the human population. Apparently, the normal sources of food for the animals are depleted through the war's destruction. The animals, crazed with hunger, will no longer fear coming into the places of human habitation and will attack and kill people in great numbers.

The Continuing Seal Judgments

In the earlier seal judgments, Antichrist presented himself in disguise as a peacemaker, to take over nations. When this attempt to seize nations through deceit was thwarted, the Antichrist initiated World War I of the Tribulation, a war to conquer the world. This results in millions of people dying through warfare, famine, pestilence, and even attacks from wild animals. Yet, ultimately, he conquers the entire known world (Rev. 13:7).

The seal judgments also include the fifth seal in Revelation 6:9–11 which is the persecution of the saints. As a result of the war of Gog and Magog, as well as an angel sent to proclaim the Gospel and two witnesses who arise with a powerful ministry, millions of people come to believe the Gospel of Jesus Christ and become believers or are saved and converted to Jesus during this time.

Yet, the Antichrist targets these people and kills all he can find. As a result, this seal shows a scene where millions of souls are seen under the throne of God, martyred for their faith, and crying out to God for Him to bring judgment on the Antichrist.

The sixth seal in Revelation 6:12–17 includes an earthquake that will affect the entire world to such an extent that many people will flee for their lives, and even the wealthy people will run to hide in the mountains and caves to try to escape the wrath of God that has come. This terrible judgment will include the great earthquake, the sun turning black, the moon becoming like blood, the stars falling to the Earth, and the sky splitting apart like a scroll. Then will follow the Trumpet Judgments.

The Trumpet Judgments

When Jesus opens the seventh seal in Revelation 8:1, there is such a shock at the coming of the calamity and severity of judgment that there is silence in Heaven for half an hour. This seventh seal encapsulates or opens the seven trumpet judgments.

These trumpet judgments are given in Revelation 8:7–9:23 and we can see the intensity of God's judgment increasing.

1. The first trumpet judgment in Revelation 8:1 brings "hail and fire mingled with blood." One-third of the trees and all grass are burned (Joel 2:30–31). Obviously, an ecological disaster occurs.

2. The second trumpet sounds in Revelation 8:8–9. At its blast, a burning mountain (or giant asteroid or meteor) decimates one-third of the sea creatures and one-third of the ships, destroying one-third of the salt water.

3. The third trumpet in Revelation 8:10–11 summons a great meteor called "wormwood." It poisons one-third of the fresh waters and fills the air with poisons like acid rain.

4. The fourth trumpet is given in Revelation 8:12. With its sounding, the sun, moon, and stars are smitten, and one-third of light is diminished like a nuclear winter. At this time, an angel will fly through the heavens announcing three greater woes will follow.

5. The fifth trumpet of Revelation 9:1–12 heralds the first woe. A mighty angel with the key to the

bottomless pit opens it and out comes living locusts, scorpion-like demons that torment men for five months with dreadful stings. These demons afflict only humans, not nature. They are permitted to harm only those people who do not have the "seal of God in their forehead."

Although their victims will suffer and long for death (Rev. 9:6), their wishes will not be granted. These locust-like and scorpion-like demons come from the same "bottomless pit" into which Satan will later be cast and confined for a thousand years.

6. The sounding of the sixth trumpet in Revelation 9:13-21 introduces a second terrible woe in which four fallen angels are loosed from the river Euphrates and they lead 200 million more invading demons. These demons inflict unbearable pain and death and will kill one-third of mankind. What a devastating plague of immense proportions will fall on wicked men.

7. After the second woe judgment passes, there is a clear division in the book of Revelation (Rev. 11:14). This brings the seventh trumpet and the announcement, *"The kingdoms of this world have become the kingdoms of our Lord and of his Christ"* (Rev. 11:15). In other words, the final judgments to come will be the end of God's wrath and righteousness and the rule of God will be restored to the Earth. This seventh trumpet includes the final vial judgments of Revelation 12-19.

The seventh trumpet judgment is also the third woe judgment. The third woe is revealed after the seventh trumpet judgment. This woe is parallel to the trumpet that sounds in Joel 2 and it signals the consummation of God's plan for the entire world. The final woe marks the finishing of God's judgment on sin and this includes judgment continuing until the kingdom of God comes at Christ's coming and this kingdom is established on the Earth.

The third woe contains the final bowl judgments (Rev. 16:1–21) and will be the greatest horror the world has ever seen. Jesus reminds us, that *"except those days should be shortened; there should no flesh be saved"* (or if the days had not been shortened, no one would survive) (Matt. 24:22).

As a result, we can see that this World War I of the Tribulation will include the aftermath of war, which is disease, famine, and death, even the attack of wild animals. But it will also include the destruction of one-third of the trees and grass, of one-third of the salt water with the death of fish and destruction of ships, the destruction of one-third of the fresh water, and the decimation of the skies with the reduction of one-third of the light from the sun, moon, and stars.

Additional judgments include the coming of two groups of demons. The first scorpion-like demons will inflict pain on unbelievers for five months and the second 200 million demons will inflict pain and death on an additional third of mankind.

Will Nuclear War Be a Possibility?

Dr. David Reagan believes that World War I of the Tribulation will bring about a multitude of judgments on nature and man. However, he also has an unusual view. He believes that the Seal judgments are a conventional war fought by the Antichrist, but during the Trumpet judgments, there are nuclear aspects or there will be nuclear warfare, and that the second half of the Antichrist's war is a nuclear war.

Dr. Reagan explains:

> The Trumpet Judgments appear to be a continuation of the conventional war launched by Antichrist

to conquer the world. But it appears that the trumpet judgments are the result of the conventional war of the Seal judgment morphing into a war of a different dimension, resulting in a nuclear holocaust.[96]

As evidence of this view, he points to the hail and fire coming from heaven that destroy one-third of the trees and grass, the great mountain thrown into the sea to destroy one-third of sea life and shipping, and the great star that falls to Earth and destroys one-third of the fresh water of the world.

Noted author, Dr. Hal Lindsey agrees. He tells us:

> Although it is possible for God to supernaturally pull off every miracle in the book of Revelation and use totally unheard-of means to do it, I personally believe that all the enormous ecological catastrophes described in this chapter (Revelation 8) are the direct use of nuclear weapons. In actuality, man inflicts these judgments on himself. God simply steps back and removes His restraining influence from man, allowing him to do what comes naturally out of his sinful nature. In fact, if the book of Revelation had never been written, we might predict these very catastrophes within fifty years or less![97]

It is certainly possible for God to bring these judgments through supernatural means as He unleashes His wrath on man, but He may choose to let the evil of man grow to the point of the use of nuclear weapons. Whether God uses conventional warfare, nuclear warfare, or just unleashes His supernatural wrath on man is unclear, but this time of war will be unparalleled in death and destruction.

---

96. David R. Reagan, *9 Wars of the End Times*, p. 75.

97. Hal Lindsey, *There's a New World Coming: A Prophetic Odyssey* (Irvine, CA: Harvest House Publishers, 1973), p. 130.

The Scale of Death in the First Half of Tribulation

The current world population in February 2025 is over 8.2 billion people according to the United Nations.[98] The deaths resulting from the seal judgments of this war will be unprecedented with one-fourth of the world's population killed (Rev. 6:8). With our current world population, that would total over 2 billion people killed in the first part of the three and a half years.

The Bible then tells us in Revelation 9:32 that an additional one-third of mankind is killed during the trumpet judgments. If the aftermath of the seal judgments has killed over 2 billion people and there are about 6 billion people left on Earth, then the Trumpet judgments will kill an additional one-third of the Earth's population or an additional 2 billion people.

The total death toll would equal about 4 billion people by the middle of the Tribulation or one-half of the total population of the world. This death and destruction is unheard of in all of human history.

---

98. www.Worldometer.info, Accessed on August 17, 2024.

CHAPTER TEN

ADDITIONAL TRIBULATION WARS

The Antichrist's Middle East War

Another war occurs on Earth in the middle of the Tribulation period. This war is mentioned in Daniel 11:36-45. While this war primarily concerns the Antichrist and his attack on three nations and it deals with the Middle East region, it is worldwide in impact, especially as it changes the structure of the one-world government, so this war will be called World War II of the Tribulation.

The first thirty-five verses of Daniel 11 deal with the prophecy that details the Jewish oppression by Persian and Grecian kings in the years that led up to the New Testament. This especially climaxed in the oppression of the Jews by Antiochus Epiphanes, a Seleucid king who ruled Israel from 215 BC to 164 BC. This evil ruler is a prophetic type of the Antichrist in Daniel 11:21-35.

In earlier times, Antiochus desecrated the Jewish Temple before Jesus gave the prophecy in Matthew 24:15 of desecration in future times in the latter days. This earlier Temple desecration by Antiochus included setting up pagan altars to sacrifice to pagan gods and it also included the sacrifice of a pig on the altar.

This sacrilege was especially repugnant to the Jewish population and it was done as an insult to the Jewish people. Similarly, this future Temple desecration in the latter days is seen as the ultimate event of extreme evil to the Jewish people and their Temple and it will signal the Jews to flee the Antichrist.

The One-World Government

In the latter days just prior to the Tribulation period, the world has developed into a one-world government, it has been separated into ten kingdoms and ten kings arise to jointly rule the Earth. This had earlier been prophesied in Daniel 7:7–8 and verses 23–24.

In chapter seven of Daniel, the prophet is telling of the future Gentile empires. He had earlier described Babylon, Medo-Persia, Greece, and the Roman empires, but in the latter days this fourth beast, or last form of one-world government rule, will be markedly different. Daniel describes the last kingdom as the fourth beast which had ten horns, or ten kings. From these nations came another "little horn" or king who eventually rises to take over the other kingdoms, and this little horn will be the Antichrist.

Daniel 7:7–8 says:

> *After this I saw in the night visions, and behold a fourth beast, dreadful and terrible, and strong exceedingly; and it had great iron teeth: it devoured and brake in pieces, and stamped the residue with the feet of it: and it was diverse from all the beasts that were before it; and it had ten horns. I considered the horns, and, behold, there came up among them another little horn, before whom there were three of the first horns plucked up by the roots: and, behold, in this horn were eyes like the eyes of man, and a mouth speaking great things.*

Later, in the chapter, Daniel repeats and explains the earlier verses. Daniel 7:23–24 says:

> *Thus he said, The fourth beast shall be the fourth kingdom upon earth, which shall be diverse from all kingdoms, and shall devour the whole earth, and shall tread it down, and break it in pieces. And the ten horns*

out of this kingdom are ten kings that shall arise: and another shall rise after them; and he shall be diverse from the first, and he shall subdue three kings.

Thus, we can see that the world's last empire will develop into the one-world government and that this kingdom will be divided into ten kingdoms or ten regions of the world. In each kingdom or region, a king or ruler will oversee that part of the world.

The Antichrist will come from this ten-kingdom alliance and become the most powerful of the rulers as an eleventh king, later coming to challenge the ten kings. In the middle of the Tribulation, the Antichrist will move to take full control of all ten kingdoms and will become the supreme ruler of the entire world.

This future Middle East war is the event that he uses to accomplish full world control and dominion.

The Character of the Antichrist

In Daniel 11, there is a shift in the narrative in verse 36. Now, the prophet Daniel describes a future king who will "do according to his will." Thus, the Antichrist is also called the Willful King, and his character is described in Daniel 11:36–39,

And the king shall do according to his will; and he shall exalt himself, and magnify himself above every god, and shall speak marvellous things against the God of gods, and shall prosper till the indignation be accomplished: for that that is determined shall be done. Neither shall he regard the God of his fathers, nor the desire of women, nor regard any god: for he shall magnify himself above all. But in his estate shall he honour the God of forces: and a god whom his fathers knew not shall he honour with gold, and silver, and with precious stones, and pleasant things. Thus shall he do in the most strong holds with a strange god, whom he shall acknowledge and increase with glory: and he shall cause them to rule over many, and shall divide the land for gain.

These verses tell us that the Antichrist will be full of pride and magnify himself above all gods of Earth; he will do according to his will and accomplish anything he desires. He will not regard the God of his fathers, which some interpret as the God of Abraham, Isaac, and Jacob, or the God of the Bible.

From this verse, some believe that Antichrist is Jewish, while others hold that he even claimed to be a Christian at the beginning of his reign. Whatever the case, Antichrist soon kills Christian believers, and in the middle of the Tribulation, moves to kill the Jews also.

Also, the Antichrist does not desire women, which would be viewed, especially in a society that follows the Bible and has a moral conscious, as an extremely odd and evil man. He will probably be a proud homosexual and follow extreme moral perversion.

Antichrist will *"exalt himself, and magnify himself above every god"* (verse 36), he *"shall speak marvellous things against the God of gods"* (verse 36), he will not show *"regard* [for] *any god"* (verse 37), and he will *"magnify himself above all"* (verse 38).

At this time, he will also personally worship a god of forces, which may be a demonic power. And he will divide the world into sectors and strategies for his personal gain.

These verses of Daniel 11:36–39 describe a future leader. They do not describe Antiochus of past history but another coming king and this king's actions in verses 40–45 were also not done by Antiochus but await fulfillment with another future king.

The Details of the Daniel 11 Middle East War

Now, at this time, the Antichrist will fight the kings of the Middle East. He moves to take control of the world, but some nations have already begun to rebel and there are movements to revolt. Daniel 11:40–45 gives us the scene,

And at the time of the end shall the king of the south push at him: and the king of the north shall come against him like a whirlwind, with chariots, and with horsemen, and with many ships; and he shall enter into the countries, and shall overflow and pass over. He shall enter also into the glorious land, and many countries shall be overthrown; but these shall escape out of his hand, even Edom, and Moab, and the chief of the children of Ammon. He shall stretch forth his hand also upon the countries: and the land of Egypt shall not escape. But he shall have power over the treasures of gold and silver, and over all the precious things of Egypt: and the Libyans and the Ethiopians shall be at his steps. But tidings out of the east and out of the north shall trouble him: therefore he shall go forth with great fury to destroy, and utterly to make away many. And he shall plant the tabernacles of his palace between the seas in the glorious holy mountain; yet he shall come to his end, and none shall help him.

The Rebellion of the Middle East Kings

The Antichrist is provoked into war by the king of the south, who historically is always Egypt, and the king of the north, which is Syria. The Antichrist will reveal that he wants to rule all of the world, and his alliance with the ten kings is shattered.

He then moves against the king of the south (Egypt), the king of the north (Syria), and the king of the east (Mesopotamia) which is Iraq. Antichrist conquers all of the Middle

Eastern nations at this time and kills these three kings. When he defeats and kills the first three kings, all of the other kings submit to his rulership.

By conquering Egypt, he has opened the door to conquer all of Africa. By conquering Mesopotamia (Iraq), he opened the door to all of the land of India and the Far East. By conquering Syria, he gains a foothold in the area near Turkey, and southeastern Europe.

Antichrist takes the riches of each country he conquers, such as the gold and silver of Egypt, and he becomes immensely wealthy and has the money to continue to expand his world domination and follow his wicked desires. During this time, Antichrist comes to "the glorious land," Daniel's description of Israel, and he makes this his home base of operations. Antichrist will make his home base between the two seas (the Mediterranean Sea and the Dead Sea) at the holy mountain. In other words, he will be based in Jerusalem at the Temple Mount for this war.

The Death of the Antichrist

Apparently, during the fighting of this Middle East war, the Antichrist is killed. This could also come about through a military coup, murder, or assassination, but the death of Antichrist occurs. Notice the end of Daniel 11:45, *"yet he shall come to his end, and none shall help him."*

This death of the Antichrist is further explained in Revelation 13:3-4: *"And I saw one of his heads as it were wounded to death; and his deadly wound was healed: and all the world wondered after the beast. And they worshipped the dragon which gave power unto the beast: and they worshipped the beast, saying, Who is like unto the beast? who is able to make war with him?"*

Here, *"one of his heads as it was wounded to death"* refers to the Antichrist. He was one of the leaders of the ten-nation alliance referred to in Revelation 13:1. At this point, the one-world government has risen to power and Antichrist is one of the heads of government.

As he moves to take control of the entire world, he fights the other kings. During this conflict, Antichrist is killed and comes back to life. Sometimes, this is thought to mean that Antichrist appeared to die, but did not actually die.

The phrase *"as it was wounded to death"* is also translated *"as though it had been smitten unto death."* So, some interpreters believe this means that Antichrist did not die but only appeared to die.

But this same phrase is also used of Jesus dying on the cross in Revelation 5:6. In describing Jesus, this verse says, *"...stood a Lamb as it had been slain."* Yet, we know Jesus died on the cross and was dead for three days and nights before His resurrection.

Dr. Fruchtenbaum tells us: "This is simply an idiom for a resurrected individual and real death is involved. So, in the course of this conflict between the Antichrist and the other ten kings, the Antichrist is killed."[99]

At this point, the events of Revelation 12:7–12 occur. While war breaks out on Earth between the Antichrist and the ten kings, war will also break out in the atmospheric heavens (Rev. 12:7). As a result of this war, Satan is cast out of Heaven and confined to Earth. This spiritual war is next explained in more detail. And then the other events of the Middle East war continue.

The War in Heaven

At this point of the Tribulation, a new series of fighting occurs, but this is instituted through a spiritual battle in Heaven, not a physical war on Earth. Since the fall of Satan described in Isaiah 14, Satan has ruled this world

---
99. Fruchtenbaum, *The Footsteps of Messiah*, p. 165.

and tempted man from the time of his creation.

During the Tribulation, the Antichrist has risen to power and finally gained control of the world. The Antichrist is Satan-possessed and fully controlled by Satan and now the Antichrist moves to kill the Jews and completely remove the Jewish race from the face of the Earth.

This renewed call for the death of the Jewish people is satanically inspired and is based on a spiritual battle in Heaven. Daniel 12:1 gives us the scene: *"And at that time shall Michael stand up, the great prince which standeth for the children of thy people: and there shall be a time of trouble, such as never was since there was a nation even to that same time: and at that time thy people shall be delivered, every one that shall be found written in the book."*

In this verse, when the Jewish people are suddenly put in distress, savagely attacked, and flee for their lives, the archangel Michael comes to their rescue as their protector. During the second half of the Tribulation, great distress will fall on the Jewish people, but Michael will fight for them and protect them. This battle is also described in more detail in Revelation 12.

Revelation 12:1-6 says:

> *And there appeared a great wonder in heaven; a woman clothed with the sun and the moon under her feet, and upon her head a crown of twelve stars: And she being with child cried, travailing in birth, and pained to be delivered. And there appeared another wonder in heaven; and behold a great red dragon, having seven heads and ten horns, and seven crowns upon his heads. And his tail drew the third part of the stars of heaven, and did cast them to the earth: and the dragon stood before the woman which was ready to be delivered, for to devour her child as soon as it was born. And she brought forth a man child, who was to rule all nations with a rod*

of iron: and her child was caught up unto God, and to his throne. And the woman fled into the wilderness, where she hath a place prepared of God, that they should feed her there a thousand two hundred and threescore days.

The Spiritual Battle Between Satan and Christ

In this passage of Revelation 12, the birth of the Messiah, Jesus Christ, is portrayed and Satan as a dragon is waiting for the birth to kill the baby who will be the Savior. Yet, Jesus is supernaturally delivered from Satan and harm and taken to Heaven.

Jesus is the man-child Satan wants to devour while the nation of Israel is the remnant of the seed of the woman. The twelve stars of the woman's crown are the twelve tribes and the woman is Israel because Christ was born of Israel. The sufferings of the woman refer to Israel as a whole and the difficulties of Israel in history as they are awaiting the birth of Messiah.

After Jesus' first coming and time on Earth, He was taken up to Heaven and is at the throne of God until His Second Coming. This man-child will later rule the world with a rod of iron, meaning He will be the supreme ruler of the world and will arbitrate justice with a rod of iron, or with all power and authority.

The Jews Flee to Petra

The woman will meanwhile flee into the mountains to a place prepared for her. Interestingly, there is a city just east and south of Jerusalem in southern Jordan that has the Greek name of Petra (or Rock), also known in Hebrew as Bozrah. This ancient city is 267 kilometers or about 165 miles south of Jerusalem. But because of crossing national borders and crossing the unusual terrain, it takes about five to six hours of travel by car or bus.

This is the location of the ancient Edomite kingdom, and later, the Nabataean kingdom, and was an ancient city built into a mountain that is twenty square miles of underground ruins. This uninhabited city is full of ancient ruins that could hold large numbers of people who could reside in the earlier underground chambers.

This city also has a Roman theatre that holds eighty-five hundred, and the city is estimated to have had a population of thirty thousand people in Roman times. While this is currently a popular tourist destination, the city and region are uninhabited today and could easily hold vast numbers of Jewish people hiding from the Antichrist. Thus, the Jews will flee to Petra during this time.

Satan Is Cast to Earth

Revelation 12:7 says:

> *And there was war in heaven: Michael and his angels fought against the dragon; and the dragon fought and his angels, And prevailed not; neither was their place found any more in heaven. And the great dragon was cast out, that old serpent, called the Devil, and Satan, which deceiveth the whole world: he was cast out into the earth, and his angels were cast out with him.*

This is the time of the Great Tribulation (the more intense second half of the Tribulation period) prophesied by Jesus in Matthew 24 and is marked by the war in Heaven. In this war, Michael and his angels fight against the dragon and his angels.

The dragon and his angels are not strong enough to overcome and they are cast out of Heaven. Satan is cast to Earth with his angels and then he leads the Earth astray (Rev. 12:7–9). Satan then attacks and pursues Israel but they are saved by the Lord. The major consequence of this war is that Satan is confined to Earth.

Satan's access to Heaven is removed and he is no longer able to stand before the Throne of God and accuse the brethren. This causes great rejoicing in Heaven (Rev. 17:10–12a). Because of this restriction, Satan is full of wrath, knowing his time is short, and he only has three and a half years left to torment man and accomplish his evil purpose. This satanic wrath is woe for Earth and will be the evil of the middle and second half of the tribulation.

This war of Heaven happens just before the middle of the Tribulation because the Jews flee the Antichrist and his persecution for three and a half years. Jesus had already told us that the abomination of desolation would occur in the middle of the Tribulation (Matt. 24:15) and this is the time when the Jews will flee the Antichrist.

The Resurrection of the Antichrist

As Satan has been confined to Earth, he now moves to kill all of the Jewish people. To accomplish this, he uses the two beasts of Revelation 13. He begins this course by bringing the Antichrist back to life as mentioned in Revelation 13:3: *"And I saw one of his heads as it were wounded to death; and his deadly wound was healed: and all the world wondered after the beast."*

Because Antichrist had been killed, he was raised to life and this brought the admiration and worship of the people. The False Prophet also promoted the worship of Antichrist. Antichrist was raised to life to become the supreme leader of the world and to help accomplish the goals of Satan.

Yet, again, the question is sometimes asked, was Antichrist actually raised from death? Again, Dr. Fruchtenbaum tells us:

The idiom [as it was wounded to death] refers to a resurrected individual. The person was killed and by all human experience should have been dead. But suddenly he is very much alive because of resurrection. The text goes on to say that his death stroke was healed, that is, by resurrection.

Satan will raise the Antichrist from death to accomplish his evil goals. He will give full authority and power to the Antichrist and then the Antichrist will move to possess all the nations and kingdoms of this world.

The Death of the Three Kings Result in the Submission of the World

The Antichrist will ultimately accomplish this world domination through his Middle East War to take full possession of the world. After the resurrection of the Antichrist, he will quickly take power of his forces and continue the war with the three Middle Eastern kings.

Daniel 7:24 tells us: *"And the ten horns out of this kingdom are ten kings that shall arise: and another shall rise after them; and he shall be diverse from the first, and he shall subdue three kings."*

This means that the Antichrist will arise after the ten-king political alliance has become the one-world government. He will be a different leader from the other ten world leaders and he will subdue or overcome three of the ten kings. This time is explained in more detail in Revelation 17:10–13.

> *And there are seven kings: five are fallen, and one is, and the other is not yet come; and when he cometh, he must continue a short space. And the beast that was, and is not, even he is the eighth, and is of the seven, and goeth*

into perdition. And the ten horns which thou sawest are ten kings, which have received no kingdom as yet; but receive power as kings one hour with the beast. These have one mind, and shall give their power and strength unto the beast.

Of these seven kings, the one that is coming last will continue to rule the world for only a short time (verse 10). The text says this beast was, and is not, and is the eighth king (verse 11). This is the eighth king who was killed and risen and becomes the eighth world ruler and, in the end, he "goeth into perdition," or he goes to Hell. He is called the "son of perdition" in 2 Thessalonians 2:3, and he is seen as a leader led by his father, the devil. He will eventually go to meet Satan in Hell. This is part of an evil trinity of Satan, the Antichrist, and the False Prophet.

These kings all rise to power with the rise of the one-world government at the same time as the Beast, or the Antichrist (Rev. 17:12; 13:1–4). All of the kings of the one-world government will join with the Antichrist, and after he has killed three of the kings, the other seven kings will submit to his authority and leadership.

They will also agree completely with all his tyrannical rulings and maniacal judgments and have the "same mind" (Rev. 17:12). These seven kings will support the Antichrist in any evil endeavor and in every decision he makes to control the world. This will include his move to change laws and times, institute his worship, and kill all believers and Jews. They will give "their power and strength unto the beast," meaning they will support and enforce his evil leadership to bring about the most evil dictatorship of all of Earth's history.

Because the Antichrist has been based in Jerusalem from the Temple Mount itself, the center of Israel's historic worship of God, and because he has now overcome all opposition and become the supreme leader of the world, he will rise up in extreme pride and think of himself as a god. And this will lead to his desecration of the Temple.

The Antichrist's Demand for Worship

The Antichrist has been concentrating on conquering the world and this has occupied his attention. But after this World War I of the Tribulation is accomplished and he has conquered the nations he desires, and after the rebellion and war with the Middle East nations, then Antichrist will move to begin his worship of self as the god of this world. He not only desires to be the supreme ruler, emperor, and king of the Earth but to be the god of all the Earth as well.

The Antichrist Will Consider Himself the god of This World

The Antichrist has come to Jerusalem to set up his religious worship and take his place as god of this world, demanding worship in the Jewish Temple. This is the time when the Antichrist will break his covenant with Israel, enter the Jewish Temple, and desecrate it (Dan. 8:24; 11:36; 2 Thess. 2:3–4).

He will enter the Holy of Holies, throw out the Ark of the Covenant, and place a statue of himself in its place. At this time, the Antichrist will be seated in the Temple and the False Prophet will call the people to come to the Temple and worship the Antichrist as god (Rev. 13).

The False Prophet will also do signs and wonders to encourage the worship of Antichrist, such as making the statue appear to come to life and to speak. All people who would not worship the Antichrist are condemned to death (Rev. 13:12–15). Of course, this is an attempt of Satan to be worshiped by man on Earth as god.

The Jews have previously been told that when they

see this abomination of desolation occur, to flee to the mountains and many people will flee and go into hiding. When the Jews see this desecration of their Temple by Antichrist, they will be outraged and immediately revolt and reject him as their political leader. This will be a revolt of the entire nation and will cause confusion in Antichrist's world empire.

The Antichrist Will Move to Kill the Jews

This event will probably shock Antichrist who is completely full of pride and cannot imagine why anyone, especially the Jewish people, would want to reject him as god. They would have lived in a covenant of peace for three and a half years in Israel while all of the rest of the nations of the world would have lived in war.

During the previous three and a half years, the Jewish people had lived in peace and safety under this peace agreement of the Antichrist, while the rest of the Gentile world had a worldwide war of the Antichrist's conquests. So great was the carnage and death that it is estimated that half of the world's Gentile population have been killed by this time.

With over four billion Gentile deaths while Israel was living in peace, now the Antichrist with great fury and vigor will turn to kill all the Jewish population. Whether he hates the Jews because of their lack of loyalty to him after their earlier agreement of national peace and lack of war and death, or he hates them because they rejected him as god on Earth, he suddenly turns on the Jewish people with vengeance.

Only in Israel have the people lived in safety and lacked great death with war, and now the Antichrist will bring that death to the Jewish people. He will be obsessed with destroying them; that is his primary goal in the second half of the Tribulation (Rev. 13:7).

During this period, God will unleash the seven vial or bowl judgments which will lead to the final and greatest battle of all Earth's existence, the Campaign of Armageddon.

The Seven Bowl Judgments

In Revelation 15, the second half of the Tribulation continues with the judgments of the bowls of wrath. This is when God continues to pour out judgment on this world, and during this time, it is intensified.

In Revelation 15, the angels in Heaven bring forth the bowl judgments to carry out the final series of judgments.

- The first bowl judgment (Rev. 16:2) affects those on Earth who have taken the mark of the beast. Previously, the Antichrist (or Beast) had required everyone to take his mark of 666 on their right arm or forehead to show allegiance to him and to buy and sell (Rev. 13:16–18). Now, those who have this mark will have a grievous sore of a skin ailment as a judgment of their worship of the Antichrist.

- The second bowl judgment (Rev. 16:3) affects the sea life. In the earlier second trumpet judgment, a part of the salt sea life was affected. Now, the remainder of sea life is affected as the rest of the salt sea is turned to blood.

- The third bowl judgment (Rev. 16:4–7) affects the rest of the fresh water. The earlier third trumpet had affected part of the world's fresh water, now under the third judgment, the remainder of rivers and springs will be affected. Some people believe the water in cisterns and wells will survive but the main sources of fresh water will turn to blood. Those who have persecuted the prophets and saints are now given blood to drink.

- The fourth bowl judgment (Rev. 16:8) affects the skies. The earlier fourth trumpet judgment had affected the sun and this judgment will increase the heat of the sun to scorch men on the Earth. Realizing this increased heat is a judgment of God, instead of returning to God, they will blaspheme His name.
- The fifth bowl judgment (Rev. 16:10-11) includes a worldwide blackout. The earlier trumpet judgment was the third worldwide blackout. All of the kingdom of Antichrist will be darkened and there will be no light on Earth except in the region of Jordan where the Jews are hiding.
- The sixth and seventh bowl judgments are connected to Armageddon.
- The sixth bowl judgment (Rev. 16:12-16) is the drying up of the Euphrates River. This is done to allow the Antichrist's forces to come more easily to Israel from the area of Babylon. The kings of the east are the leaders of Babylon and Assyria which would be the area of Iraq and Syria and these kings also lead their armies to Armageddon.

During this time, the political and economic center of Antichrist and his world headquarters will be on the banks of the Euphrates River in Babylon, or in modern Iraq. This is the capital city of the one-world government of Antichrist. Babylon will be the center of Antichrist's power and this city is also the location of much of his armed forces. Antichrist will then move his Iraqi-based forces to Armageddon.

This gathering of the Antichrist's forces is demonic, led by three demons, and will also involve the work of Satan, the Antichrist and the False Prophet who will lead the armies to Armageddon working signs. The seven kings previously under the rule of Antichrist prepare their armies to fight and bring them to the valley of Armageddon and they are joined by armies of the entire world.

- The seventh bowl judgment (Rev. 16:17–21) brings a great earthquake and a tremendous storm of hailstones as the people are plagued with hail and disrupted by a huge earthquake. This will occur during the time of Armageddon.

Jerusalem is divided into three parts by this earthquake. The city of Babylon will be filled with the wrath of God, there will be many geographical changes, and hail will fall weighing one hundred twenty pounds (Rev. 16:17–21).

During the Tribulation, the judgment of God has continued to grow in intensity and severity, as these judgments lead to the most climatic and dramatic of all events. The bowl judgments ultimately bring about the most stupendous of all the world's wars, the Campaign of Armageddon.

CHAPTER ELEVEN

THE CAMPAIGN OF ARMAGEDDON

Coming to the world is a world war that is so staggering in size and scope and so tremendous in final destruction that the very word Armageddon has become synonymous with the complete annihilation and end of the world. Although most people have never heard of many of these future wars in the Bible, almost everyone has heard of the word Armageddon as some terrible destruction and end of the world.

Yet, usually, people know very little about what Armageddon actually means, when it occurs, and what are the events involved.

The name, Armageddon, is found in the description of a war where the kings of the entire world are drawn by evil spirits and demons and they gather to battle at the place of Armageddon. This is mentioned in Revelation 16:14 and 16: *"For they are the spirits of devils, working miracles, which go forth unto the kings of the earth and of the whole world, to gather them to the battle of that great day of God Almighty. ... And he gathered them together into a place called in the Hebrew tongue Armageddon."*

The location of this conflict is known today by the later version of this name as Megiddo, from the Hebrew name which means *Mount Megiddo*. The ruins of an ancient city and fortress have been found that go back to the time near the flood of Noah. Twenty-five ancient cities were rebuilt on the same site until a large hill or tell of ruins remain which marks the location. This was an ancient Canaanite city, and later the fortress city of King Solomon and later still of King Ahab.

This ancient city sits at the southern edge of the valley of *Jezreel* which means "God saves." The valley of Jezreel sits at the top of a much larger valley called the Valley of Megiddo. In the middle of the valley was an important trade route, The Way of the Sea, the *Via Maris*, and this city was part of the trade route and a fortress to protect the movement of caravans and travelers of trade. Megiddo and Armageddon actually refer to the ancient city, not the valley, but this valley has come to be associated with the war.

In this valley, Deborah and Barak defeated the Canaanites (Judges 4:1–16) and Gideon defeated the Midianites (Judges 7). Here was also the defeat and death of King Saul and Jonathan (1 Sam. 31:1–2) and the later death of King Josiah (2 Kings 23:29, 2 Chron. 35:22–24).

This farming area continued to be a battlefield throughout history. Here, Sultan Saladin defeated the Crusaders in 1187 and 1189, the Egyptian Mamelukes defeated the invading Mongols in 1260 and stopped their advance into the West, Napoleon defeated the Turks in 1799, General Allenby defeated the Ottoman Turks and Germans in 1918 during World War I, and the Israelis fought the Arabs in 1948, 1967 and 1973.[100]

Yet, even the name of the conflict, the Battle of Armageddon, is not correct because no fighting happens in this place and there are several events, not just one battle. For that reason, many commentators now refer to this as the Campaign of Armageddon, although it is more accurately *"the battle of that great day of God Almighty."*

This can also be called World War III of the Tribulation because it is truly a world war in the involvement of all nations and the scope of impact. This will truly be the "War to End All Wars." All of the fears of mankind of the end of the world are warranted and we should fear this

---

100. David R. Reagan, *9 Wars of the End Times*, p. 118.

war because it will be the most fearsome and terrifying war in all of history.

By the way, the 200-million-man army that some people suppose is a Chinese army coming to the battle is actually an army of demons related to the earlier trumpet judgments of Revelation 9, and the "kings of the east" are not references to the Chinese or other Asian nations but also refer to another judgment. In the Bible, the kings of the East always refer to Assyria and Babylon and never to any location in the Far East, such as China.

Far East nations are probably involved in this conflict of Armageddon because Armageddon includes all nations of the world, but they are not specifically mentioned in the Bible. Thus, the details sometimes applied to China of a rising army coming to Israel are not actually referring to China but to an earlier invasion of demons.

The Assembly of Antichrist's Forces at Armageddon

The sixth bowl judgment dries up the Euphrates River and allows for easier movement for the army in Babylon to come to Armageddon. The evil trinity of Satan, Antichrist, and the False Prophet are working to bring the world's forces to Armageddon to overcome and kill the Jews in hiding in Israel and Jordan. They use signs to make the armies of the kings comply with an order given in Revelation 16:13–14 by Antichrist for the armies to gather.

These kings who lead the forces of Armageddon are the seven kings who will rule with Antichrist (Rev. 17) and seem to be joined with armies of the entire world. There is no fighting in Armageddon, but this is the location of the gathering of the armies.

This gathering is also described mockingly from God's viewpoint. In Joel 3:6–11, he sees the armies using farming equipment for war. He sees that they are weak but pretend to be strong. They are trying to turn these farming pieces into swords, and later, in the Millennium, the swords will be turned into farm equipment.

In Psalm 2, God sees that man wants to break the cords of God's control of the world, when *"the rulers take counsel together against Jehovah, and against his anointed"* and try to kill the Jews. By fighting against the Jews, God will soon put these kings and armies in confusion. Instead of them ruling the world with evil, God will overcome them and set Jesus to rule the world in righteousness from Zion.

The Destruction of Babylon

The Bible tells us that Babylon will be rebuilt and will become the world's economic capital and it will also be Antichrist's political capital (Zech. 5:5–11). Placing an ephah in the land of Shinar (the ancient name of Babylon) means that the center of the economy will move to Babylon.

In Isaiah 13:1–5, Isaiah tells us that at the time of the Day of the Lord, forces will come to destroy the city of Babylon, and it will be so devastating that only wild animals will live in the ruins (Isaiah 13:19–22). All the inhabitants will be killed (Isaiah 14:22–23) and it will never be inhabited again (Jer. 50:21–27) because of her evil influence on other nations (Jer. 51:7–9). The city's destruction will be especially severe because of her treatment and evil deeds against the people of Israel (Jer. 51:24, 35–36, 48–49).

Just prior to God's destruction of Babylon, a warning will be given to the Jews living there to flee. They will flee to Jerusalem and announce the destruction of Babylon (Jer. 50:6–8, 28).

The Antichrist will not be present when God destroys Babylon and he has to be told (Jer. 50:43; 51:31–32). This consequence is understood by comparing scriptures that he is meeting with the armies in Armageddon preparing to destroy the Jews when he is told of the fall of Babylon.

Revelation 18:6–8 tells us of the destruction of Babylon. The city is condemned to receive double the punishment inflicted on others (verse 6). Babylon will have a quick and sudden destruction by fire (verse 8) similar in severity to Sodom and Gomorrah. As a result, intense mourning will be given by those who invested heavily in Babylon and are now bankrupt (Rev. 18:9–19). The seven ruling kings will see the destruction from afar, meaning they will see the smoke of the destruction and will realize that their political kingdoms are now lost.

Being the world's economic center, the merchants will mourn the loss of the city, their loss of trade, and the loss of all their wealth in one swift moment (Rev. 18:11–17). And the people of transportation and shipping will also mourn (Rev. 18:17–19).

But while people mourn the destruction of Babylon, there will be rejoicing in Heaven by saints, apostles, and prophets (Rev. 18:20). The city of Babylon will also become a habitation for demons and their confinement during the Messianic Age (Rev. 18:1–3). No one will ever live there again; it will be the dwelling place of demons.

The Fall of Jerusalem

Although Antichrist will be at Armageddon when he hears of the destruction of Babylon, he does not go to the east to attack the forces who came there to attack his city but instead turns south to kill the Jews in Jerusalem (Zech. 12:1–3). As a result, Jerusalem will fall into the hands of the Antichrist and his forces. Half of the city will be put in slavery while the other half will await their fate (Zech. 14:1–2).

Earlier in the fighting, the Jews were so energized

and helped by God that they appeared to strike down the enemy like a fire that burns very dry tinder, and like a torch igniting a great flame. God will so empower the Jewish defenders that the weak will have the strength of David and the strong will appear to have the strength of the Angel of the Lord (Zech. 12:6–8).

While the Gentile armies will prepare to treat the Jews as if they were threshing wheat, the Gentiles will be threshed by the Jewish defenders (Zech. 12:11–12), but the Gentile armies will eventually prevail. After great losses, the Gentiles will plunder the Jewish homes in Jerusalem and ravage the women (Zech. 14:2).

The Armies of the Antichrist at Bozrah

Meanwhile, the main group of Jews are in hiding in Petra (the Greek name), also called Bozrah (the Hebrew name). Because the main objective is to eliminate the entire Jewish race, the armies of the world will go next from Jerusalem to Bozrah (Jer. 49:13–14; Micah 2:12). After the Antichrist's armies assemble at Bozrah, they will prepare for the events of the next three days.

The National Regeneration of Israel

There are two parts to the basis of Jesus' Second Coming. First, there must be the confession of Israel's national sin (Lev. 26:40–42; Jer. 3:11–18; Hosea 5:15), and secondly, there must be a pleading for Messiah to return (Zech. 12:10; Matt. 12:37–39). Now, as the armies of Antichrist are at Bozrah (Petra), the last three days of Armageddon may begin.

Hosea 6:1–3 tells us of the three-day time,

> *Come, and let us return into the LORD: for he hath torn, and he will heal us, he hath smitten, and he will bind us up. After two days will he revive us: in the third day*

he will raise us up, and we shall live in his sight. Then shall we know, if we follow on to know the LORD: his going forth is prepared as the morning; and he shall come unto us as the rain, as the latter and former rain upon the earth.

The Salvation of the Nation of Israel

Earlier, in Hosea 5:1-3, the Jewish leaders called for Israel to repent and confess their national sin. Probably through the study of Scripture, the ministry of the Two Witnesses and the 144,000 Jewish witnesses, the sign of Jonah or the ministry of Elijah, the leaders had come to realize that Jesus was the Messiah.

During this three-day period, these Jewish leaders are leading Israel to know the true Messiah as Jesus and to call upon the Lord. As the earlier Jewish leaders led Israel to reject Jesus during His ministry, now the current Jewish leaders lead Israel to accept and know Him. The confession of Israel's sin will last for two days as the entire nation of Israel is saved and regenerated (Hosea 6:2).

The actual prayer they pray in confession is given in Isaiah 53:1-9. Here, they admit that they believed Jesus was just an ordinary man and a criminal who died for his own sins. But they realize that He was the true Messiah, and the Lamb of God who carried the sins of others, and was smitten of God to pay for their sins, not His own sins.

By the people praying the words of Isaiah 53 in faith, the entire nation is saved and comes to believe in Jesus as their Messiah and Savior (Rom. 11:25-27).

After the Jewish nation believes in Jesus and is saved as an entire race of people, they will then pray that God saves them from the destruction of Antichrist's armies at Petra (Bozrah). This prayer for help from the Lord will be prayed by the Jews in Jerusalem and anywhere they are in hiding as they *"look upon me whom they have pierced"* and the Holy Spirit will help them realize that the crucified one, Jesus Christ, is the Savior (Zech. 12:10–13:1; Rev. 1:7).

During the three days, the Jews of Bozrah and Jerusalem will repent, confess, and believe on the Lord. Joel 2:28–32 tells of several unusual events that will occur during this time, as people see visions and prophesy, there is an outpouring of God's Spirit, and there are convolutions in the skies with the sun and moon.

Whoever calls upon the Lord will be saved from destruction and the Jews will believe in Jesus as the Messiah and Savior and will be saved. Many earlier Jews have been killed, but numerous Jews still living will believe and become a great remnant of the nation.

During this time, the false prophets telling of false teachings will be executed and killed (Zech. 13:2–6), sometimes by family members, and they will be revealed as false prophets by their scars which they carry to identify them as pagan prophets.

Zechariah 13:7–9 describes the regeneration of the nation of Israel:

> *Awake, O sword, against my shepherd, and against the man that is my fellow, saith the LORD of hosts: smite the shepherd, and the sheep shall be scattered: and I will turn my hand upon the little ones. And it shall come to pass, that in all the land, saith the Lord, two parts therein shall be cut off and die, but the third shall be left therein. And I will bring the third part through the fire, and will refine them as silver is refined, and will try them as gold is tried: they shall call on my name, and I will hear them: I will say, It is my people: and they shall say, The LORD is my God.*

These verses tell us that the remnant (a third of the Jewish people) will turn to the Lord and believe in their Messiah as Savior because of the fires of the Tribulation.

Verse seven tells us that God's Shepherd was smitten and His people were scattered throughout the world. Then through the fires of the Tribulation, two-thirds of the Jewish people will be killed but a remnant of a third of the people will survive and believe in the Lord (verses 8 and 9). God will hear their confession and save His people.

This pleading for salvation during this time by the Jews, their return to the Lord in belief, and the coming of the Lord are also detailed in Isaiah 64:1–12, Psalm 79:1–13, and Psalm 89:1–19. During this desperate time when Israel is surrounded by her enemies and the armies of the Antichrist, she will repent, confess, and call upon the Lord and be saved in the first two days, and then pray for the coming of the Lord on the third day.

The Second Coming of Christ

Jesus hears the cry of His Chosen People and He returns to save them from total destruction by Antichrist. As this is described, we will look at the place of His return and the manner of His return.

The Place of Jesus' Second Coming

While it is often assumed that Jesus will return at the Mount of Olives, this is only the first place His feet will touch the Earth. His actual return will begin with His return in the skies to fight the Antichrist and his forces at Bozrah in southern Jordan. The location is mentioned in Isaiah 34:1–7 as Bozrah, a city of Edom, and in Habakkuk 3:3 as Teman and Paran, places in the mountain range of Mount Seir in the area of Bozrah, Jordan. In Micah 2:12–13, the remnant of saved Jews is led as sheep by their King from Bozrah to safety, when He leads them in triumph to Jerusalem.

Isaiah 63:1–4 tells of Isaiah in a prophetic vision seeing a blood-stained figure approaching him in glory and splendor. He asks, *"Who is this that cometh from Edom, with dyed garments from Bozrah? this that is glorious in his apparel, travelling in the greatness of his strength? ..."*

This amazing figure answers, *"... I that speak in righteousness, mighty to save."*

This person can only be Jesus Christ because He alone is righteous and has never sinned. He is also the Mighty God of Isaiah 9 who can save His people from their sins.

Then Isaiah asks the Almighty God how He stained His glorious apparel in verses 2 to 4. *"Wherefore art thou red in thine apparel, and thy garments like him that treadeth in the winefat?"* (vs. 2).

Isaiah wants to know how his garments became stained so greatly as if he was stomping the grapes of wine to bring forth the blood or juice of the grapes. Remember that freshly squeezed grapes in the Bible are called new wine or what we know as fresh grape juice.

Jesus Christ responds that He has been in battle and redeemed His people. *"I have trodden the winepress alone, and of the people there was none with me: for I will tread them in mine anger, and trample them in my fury; and their blood shall be sprinkled upon my garments, and I will stain all my raiment. For the day of vengeance is in mine heart, and the year of my redeemed is come."*

Jesus alone overcame the forces of Antichrist. In His anger at the attack of His people, He saved His beloved people, and His garments were stained. This happened in Bozrah of Edom, or modern Petra of Jordan. Then the Bible tells us how Jesus will return.

The Manner of Jesus' Second Coming

In Revelation 19:11–16, the Apostle John the Beloved describes Jesus coming as the Judge of the wicked.

> *And I saw heaven opened, and behold a white horse; and he that sat upon him was called Faithful and True, and in righteousness he doth judge and make war. His eyes were as a flame of fire, and on his head were many crowns; and he had a name written, that no man knew, but he himself. And he was clothed in a vesture dipped in blood: and his name is called The Word of God. And the armies which were with in heaven followed him upon white horses, clothed in fine linen, white and clean. And out of his mouth goeth a sharp sword, that with it he should smite the nations: and he shall rule them with a rod of iron: and he treadeth the winepress of the fierceness and wrath of Almighty God. And he hath on his vesture and on his thigh a name written, KING OF KINGS, AND LORD OF LORDS.*

In this coming, there is a similarity with Jesus in Revelation 1, such as having a body that glows like fire. In this description, Jesus is the Judge and the Incarnate Word of God, returning to judge the nations in righteousness. He is the Faithful and True One wearing many crowns, showing that He is king over all nations, and His garments are stained with the blood of judgment in battle as in Isaiah 63:1–3.

Two armies accompany him to the battle. One is an angelic army of the hosts of the Lord (Matt. 16:27), and another is an army of the church saints who come to witness the victory of Christ over evil (Jude 14–15).

All church believers will accompany Jesus to the war of Armageddon to witness His victory but the church saints and the angels do not fight. Jesus does not need the help of angels or humans, for He alone is the victor of the battle and He alone does the fighting (Isa. 62:1–6). Jesus is the sole victor over sin, death, Hell, and the grave.

Jesus will just speak his Word to overcome the Antichrist and his forces. Verse 15 says, *"And out of his mouth goeth a sharp sword, that with it he should smite the nations. ..."*

Apparently, Jesus will speak a word of judgment and the armies will be slain. It is the author's opinion that when Jesus speaks His word, the bodies of the Antichrist's armies are cut in half, such as slaying someone with a sword, and that is why there is such carnage, blood, and death.

After Jesus is the Judge of the armies in battle, then Jesus will assume His role as King and rule the world with a rod of iron. Verse 15 continues, *"and he shall rule them with a rod of iron"* meaning there will be strict adherence to law and justice. Although God is a God of grace and mercy, He will demand strict following of the law and for people to live in a state of righteousness for His entire Millennial reign.

There is also a call for the birds and animals to come to a great feast. So great is the carnage that many birds will eat the unburied bodies of those who participated in the Campaign of Armageddon (Rev. 19:17–18, 21; Ezek. 39:17–21).

After the battle, the Gentiles will realize that God did not forsake His chosen people or cast off His people forever. They will know that after the Jews confessed their sin, repented, and believed on the Lord, God saved their souls and rescued His remnant of believing Jews.

Dr. Arno Fruchtenbaum states:

> The nations will recognize at the second coming of Christ that God is still Israel's God and He will avenge their affliction of Israel. For in gathering all the armies of the world against Israel, they will actually be gathering against Israel's Messiah, as Revelation

19:19 clearly states,

"*And I saw the beast, and the kings of the earth, and their armies, gathered together to make war against him that sat on the horse, and against his army.*"[101]

The Battle from Bozrah to Jerusalem

The fighting of Armageddon will begin at Bozrah and will continue all the way back to Jerusalem to the base of the current Temple mountain at the Valley of Jehoshaphat or the Kidron Valley.

Interestingly, and probably, fittingly, one of the first casualties of the war is the Antichrist. Habakkuk 3:13b tells us, "*... thou woundest the head out of the house of the wicked, by discovering the foundation unto the neck. Selah.*"

Jesus will easily defeat the Antichrist by breathing and speaking the Word of God. The Antichrist — who had claimed to be god, had done amazing signs and wonders, had ruled the entire world through the power of Satan, and had even come back from a deadly head wound and seemed to be unable to be defeated — will be effortlessly killed by Jesus. Antichrist will be killed by the breath of God and by the Word of God.

2 Thessalonians 2:8 says: "*And then shall that Wicked be revealed, whom the Lord shall consume with the spirit of his mouth, and shall destroy with the brightness of his coming.*"

Isaiah 14:3–11 tells of the Antichrist's arrival in Hell while Isaiah 14:16–21 tell us what happens to the body of the Antichrist. His dead body will be viewed in disbelief, and then trampled by his fleeing army and possibly never buried.

The fighting will continue from Bozrah to Jerusalem as these armies are treaded in the fury of the Jewish Messiah. The Bible mentions blood from the battle will stretch for sixteen hundred furlongs or two hundred miles (Rev.

---

101. Fruchtenbaum, *The Footsteps of Messiah*, p. 246.

14:15–20). This could be the distance from Armageddon to Bozrah which is about two hundred miles, or more likely the blood will run the distance from Jerusalem to the south down the Arabah valley to Eilat and Aqaba where the blood would empty into the Red Sea, which is also two hundred miles. Thus, this will be a war of great devastation and carnage and Jesus will be the victor over evil.

You can view these eight events of Armageddon on a map of the area to see where they unfold and in what order.

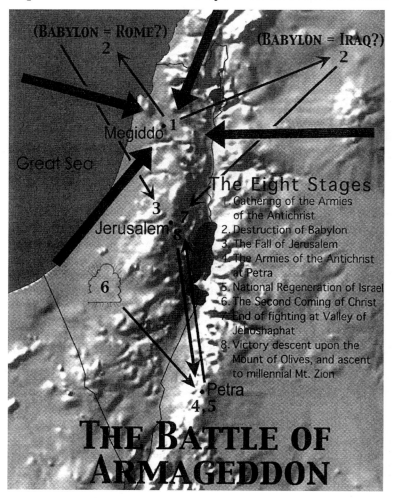

Jesus's Victory Ascent on the Mount of Olives

When the fighting has completed, Jesus will ascend up the Mount of Olives. Zechariah 14:3-4 says:

> *Then shall the LORD go forth, and fight against those nations, as when he fought in the day of battle. And his feet shall stand in that day upon the Mount of Olives, which is before Jerusalem on the east, and the mount of Olives shall cleave in the midst thereof toward the east and toward the west, and there shall be a very great valley; and half of the mountain shall remove toward the north, and half of it toward the south.*

After Jesus has fought the nations from Bozrah to Jerusalem, His feet will touch the Mount of Olives. At this moment, a series of cataclysmic events occur which are a result of the seventh bowl judgment of Revelation 16:17-21 and these events will close the Tribulation.

When the seventh bowl is poured out, a voice cries: It is finished, or It is done, meaning the judgments of the Tribulation are coming to an end. During the seventh bowl judgment, the next event is the greatest earthquake to ever occur in the history of the world (Rev. 16:18). This earthquake will divide Jerusalem into three sections, while the city of Babylon will experience the full wrath of God (Rev. 16:19). This will cause many geographical and topological changes and hail will fall weighing one hundred twenty pounds (Rev. 16:20-21).

The earthquake will shake Jerusalem and it will split into three sections. The earthquake will cause the Mount of Olives to be split in two and to fall away and make a new valley which will make a way of escape for the Jews still in Jerusalem. Then will occur the fifth worldwide blackout (Matt. 24:29; Joel 3:14-17) when the entire world is plunged again into darkness. These judgments of the seventh bowl occur during the events of Armageddon and at the end of the campaign.

The Seventy-Five-Day Interval

Next will follow a seventy-five-day interval when a number of events occur after Armageddon (Dan. 12:11-12).

There will be the removal and cleansing of the Abomination of Desolation from the Temple (Dan. 12:11). The Antichrist and the False Prophet will be cast into the lake of fire (Rev. 19:20). Satan will be bound and cast into a bottomless pit for a thousand years, but then later released a short time to test mankind one more time (Rev. 20:1-3).

Then will occur the Judgment of the Nations or the Judgment of the Gentiles, sometimes called the Judgment of the Sheep and Goats (Joel 3:1-3; Matt. 25:31-33). The *nations* mean the *Gentiles* and the Gentiles will be gathered to the Valley of Jehoshaphat for judgment.

Those Gentiles who helped the Jews in the Great Tribulation at the peril of their lives by giving them food, shelter, clothing, and visiting them will be the sheep Gentiles. These Gentiles will be allowed to enter the Millennium. They will have been the Gentiles who attacked the city of Babylon earlier and they will live to enter the Millennium. Only believing Gentiles will help the Jews in the Tribulation and only believing Gentiles will be allowed to enter the Millennium (Matt. 25:34).

There will also be the resurrection of Old Testament saints (Isa. 26:19), and the resurrection of Tribulation saints (Rev. 20:4), and these, together with the earlier resurrection of church saints at the Rapture, will complete the First Resurrection (Rev. 20:5-6).

This will bring to close the Tribulation and then the Millennial Kingdom of God will commence.

CHAPTER TWELVE

THE FUTURE KINGDOM OF GOD

After the world has experienced fighting and wars for its entire existence, peace will finally come to Earth. Jealousy, hatred, and murder started with Cain from the family of Adam, and evil so engulfed and ruled the world that all living men and animals on it were destroyed in the time of Noah with a worldwide Flood. Only Noah, his family, and a small group of each of the animals were saved in Noah's Ark. In the next world after the Flood, rebellion against God at the Tower of Babel brought the multiple languages and misunderstandings of mankind from that time forth.

The entire history of the world can then be recounted by listing its multitude of wars. When a study is made in school, we learn of the history of many wars in Egypt, Babylon, Assyria, Persia, and of Grecian, Roman, various European, Early Indo-American, African, Asian, and Asian Indian wars, as well as wars from every civilization on the planet.

Yet, mankind cannot think of a time when there was no war. There has never been a place or time of peace without war on Earth. Man has searched for peace but to no avail. Jeremiah 8:11 relates, *"For they have healed the hurt the daughter of my people slightly, saying, Peace, peace, where there is no peace."*

So, how can mankind imagine a world of peace? How can a person comprehend a world without misunderstanding, arguing, and fighting? Yet, the Bible tells us that when the Prince of Peace comes there will be an entire world ruled in righteousness and existing in peace.

Peace for Israel Is Promised through the Coming of Messiah

The entire world will change when Jesus comes. As the saying goes, "It will be a whole new world." This is because now God has come to dwell in daily fellowship with man and His presence and character change the world. As Isaiah 9:6–7 tells us:

> For unto us a child is born, unto us a son is given: and the government shall be upon his shoulder: and his name shall be called Wonderful, Counsellor, The mighty God, The everlasting Father, **The Prince of Peace. Of the increase of his government and peace there shall be no end,** upon the throne of David, and upon his kingdom, to order it, and to establish it with judgment and with justice from henceforth even for ever. The zeal of the Lord of hosts will perform this. [emphasis added].

Jesus Brings Peace to the Entire World

Jesus is coming to build a kingdom of peace. This kingdom will be established on His person. As the Wonderful One, the Counsellor with fathomless knowledge and understanding, the mighty God dwelling in the presence of mere man, the everlasting Father — literally Jehovah God and the Creator of the universe ruling on Earth, and being the Prince of Peace – the only person to bring peace to the world, Jesus alone can bring and constitute everlasting peace on Earth.

Jesus will make real and lasting peace with the removal of human oppression, and He will institute universal peace in international relations. This peace will be mirrored in the animal kingdom. There will be peace between former jealous families, between historic enemy nations, and even peace between former dangerous animals.

Wars will have stopped, fighting and violence will be forcibly quelled, and there will be no misunderstandings among nations because there will be the peace of God reigning in the hearts of men. Knowledge of the Lord will be known and His righteousness will be followed as mankind lives the principles of the Sermon on the Mount, the spiritual way of life for God's Kingdom.

This will be a kingdom of righteousness where stealing and all other forms of evil are restrained as Jesus rules the world with a rod of iron.

God has promised to make a covenant of peace with mankind. This peace will also extend to his existence with all of the world's wild animals including all former dangerous and deadly animals. Mankind will not fear or be harmed by wild animals and can sleep safely in the woods: *"And I will make with them a covenant of peace, and will cause the evil beasts to cease out of the land: and they shall dwell safely in the wilderness, and sleep in the woods"* (Ezekiel 34:25).

God's Peace Covenant with Israel

God will make a covenant with the people of Israel that will not be a temporary covenant of peace, but it will be an everlasting covenant. God will move the Jewish people to the land of Israel and to specified areas by their respective tribes. The Jewish people will multiply greatly and will live in serenity and quietness. And they will know God is back with them and watching over them because His Temple will be in their midst forevermore: *"Moreover I will make a covenant of peace with them; it shall be an everlasting covenant with them: and I will place them, and multiply them, and will set my sanctuary in the midst of them for evermore"* (Ezekiel 37:26).

This will not be a temporary peace agreement between

men but will be an everlasting covenant of peace and it will be guaranteed by the power and sovereignty of God Himself. God is righteous and holy and He cannot lie. He will accomplish His purposes and will and no man will stand against Him. When Jesus returns again, He will have the power and authority to establish a kingdom of peace and righteousness.

Peace Commences with the Return of Messiah as Savior and King

After Jesus has defeated the Antichrist and his evil forces, He will come to the Mount of Olives in triumph and free the Jews who have been trapped by an earthquake that protected them from the Antichrist during the Campaign of Armageddon. Then Jesus will ascend Mount Moriah which has now combined with Mount Zion to become a new enlarged mountain.

There, the people will build a new Temple to worship the Lord during the Millennium. Jesus will judge the nations in the new valley where the Mount of Olives once stood, and the righteous will be allowed to enter the Millennial Kingdom, while the unrighteous will be sent to begin their judgment in Hell.

Jesus will then commence his new rule of the world from the new Temple, where all the world will come to worship Him as the King of Kings, the Lord of Lords, and as the personal Savior for all who believe.

Only Jesus, the Prince of Peace, is able to *"speak peace to the nations"* (Zech. 9:10), to bring true *"peace and righteousness"* and *"turn many away from iniquity"* (Mal. 2:6). Then will follow a thousand years of true peace where *"Men shall learn war no more."* At this time, all the world will enter the Millennium as believers.

The Worship of God in the Millennium

Isaiah 2:2-4 tells us about this time:

> *And it shall come to pass in the last days, that the mountain of the LORD's house shall be established in the top of the mountains, and shall be exalted above the hills; and all nations shall flow unto it. And many people shall go and say, Come ye, and let us go up to the mountain of the LORD, to the house of the God of Jacob; and he will teach us of his ways, and we will walk in his paths: for out of Zion shall go forth the law, and the word of the LORD from Jerusalem. And he shall judge among the nations, and shall rebuke many people: and they shall beat their swords into plowshares, and their spears into pruninghooks: nation shall not lift up sword against nation, neither shall they learn war any more.*

This is the prophesied time when all the world will come to Jerusalem to worship the true God of the universe in His holy Temple. Jerusalem shall be raised up to become a great mountain, and at its peak, the Temple of God will stand as God's place of reign and worship.

At Jerusalem's Temple, the entire world will come each year to be taught the Word of God and to hear from King Jesus Himself. And the people of the world will follow the Word of God and walk in His paths.

God will judge the people and nations, will watch over their very lives, and the people will no longer need swords or spears but will turn them into daily farming and fishing tools.

The Characteristics of Christ in Millennial Peace

The longing of the believers throughout the centuries will at last be fulfilled as the righteous Judge, the holy One of Israel, the promised Deliverer, and blessed Redeemer has come to reign bodily and physically on Earth. The prophesied Messiah, the King of all Kings, has appeared as Immanuel, "God with us" (Isa. 7:14). How happy believers will be to know Jesus has come to dwell in their midst! Truly, God will dwell with man in fellowship and man will enjoy the presence of God.

From *without*, Christ will be the Uniter of His people, the Banner of the nations, and the Prince of Peace on the throne (Ezek. 37:22-24, Isa. 11:10; Luke 1:32). And from *within*, Christ is the One permeated with the Sevenfold Spirit — as the shoot out of the stem of Jesse (Isa. 11:1, 2; Rev. 5:6; 4:5), the Priest-King with the golden-silver crown, as the *Zemach*, the Branch of the Lord (Zech. 6:11-13), and the "Jehovah our righteousness" — as the Divine King and Redeemer of the world (Jer. 23:5-6; 33:15-16).

For Malachi 1:11 tells us, *"For from the rising of the sun even unto the going down of the same my name shall be great among the Gentiles; and in every place incense shall be offered unto my name, and a pure offering: for my name shall be great among the heathen, saith the LORD of hosts."*

And as Savior and King, Jesus Christ will be worshiped by all the nations of the world. People from across the world will daily have God in their lives and thinking. God will be praised as their personal Savior and Friend, as well as the God and King of the world. As one circles the Earth, one will continually find the name of God praised and honored in every place of the world, both among the Jews and the Gentiles.

The Kingdom Blessings of Israel

During the Millennial reign of Christ, all of the prophesied blessings of the covenants will come to pass. Abraham was promised a seed of immense proportions that would look like the stars in the heavens. And his progeny and offspring will come to number millions or possibly billions of people. Truly, he is a father of nations.

The Jewish people will possess all of the promised land, from the Euphrates River in the north to a tributary of the Nile River in the south, near the modern Suez Canal. This land will be divided among the tribes with a special portion for the Temple and another portion for the priests. The Kingdom of God will be centered in Israel and all the world will come to worship in Jerusalem.

The spiritual blessings of the New Covenant will be experienced by the Jewish people as God's Spirit will dwell in their hearts and minds. The Jews will also help administrate and rule the world with the Lord and lead others to righteousness. God has a special plan for His chosen people and will honor His promises to Israel.

The Conversion of the Nations Achieved in Millennial Peace

God's goal was not just to bring salvation to the Hebrews, but also to offer redemption to all mankind (1 Tim. 2:4; Isa. 40:5). As peoples and tribes, they will turn to Christ, the earlier despised Nazarene, now recognizing Him as the only true Savior and King of glory (Zech. 2:11; 8:22; 14:9; Ps. 24:7-10; Phil. 2:11; Eph. 1:10).

And God will judge the Gentiles at the judgment of the nations. Those who helped the Jews in flight from the Antichrist are found to be believers and enter the Millennium. These people will still have their natural bodies like the surviving Jews who enter the Kingdom and both groups of people will procreate and have children during the Millennium.

Although today, many people reject this offer of

salvation, during the Millennium the nations of the world will be evangelized through the message of the Kingdom, their false idols will be put down, and all human religions will vanish as Gentile nations come to the Lord. People will hear the Gospel and be saved by grace through faith, just as today.

After the judgment of the nations, Jesus will sanctify the nations and bless them by admission into the Kingdom (Joel 3:12, Matt. 25:31-46), by spiritual renewal and national conversion (Isa. 2:3; 19:21, 24-25), by political ordering (Rev. 1:5, Isa. 2:2; 45:22, 23), by international concord (Isa. 2:4; Zech. 9:10), by civil harmony (Isa. 4:2; 11:3, 9; 59:19-21), by outward happiness and inward sanctification (Zeph. 3:9; Hab. 2:14; Isa. 11:10), and by common worship of Christ (Mic. 4:2; Zech. 8:21; 14:16; Isa. 56:7; 60:3; 66:23).

The Millennial Future of the Nations

Yet, what about the nations of the Earth? What is the Millennial future of the nations of Gentiles? What happens to Israel and to her historic enemies during the Millennium?

The Bible tells of the future of the nations of the Middle East. Those nations that once fought Israel as historic enemies will now be changed and have a new future, although some nations will still carry judgment from their evil past. Because of these nations and their past hatred and fighting with Israel, God has pronounced judgments upon each country.

Nevertheless, each nation was given a specific future judgment. The results of these Arab and Middle Eastern nations usually come in one of three forms: 1) by means of occupation, 2) by means of destruction, or 3) by means of conversion.

The Future of Lebanon and Gaza

Peace will come to Lebanon by means of occupation. While Scripture does not explicitly explain this result, the Millennial boundaries of Israel include all of the land of Lebanon (Ezek. 47:13-48:29). This land will be settled by northern Israeli tribes and become a part of Israel, so Lebanon will be occupied and this is also the future result for ancient Philistia or modern Gaza.

The Future of Jordan

Modern Jordan includes the ancient kingdoms of Moab, Ammon, and Edom but the prophets were primarily concerned with Edom. There has been a long history of animosity and hatred between the people of Esau, the Edomites, and the people of Israel.

As a result of this long history of hatred, southern Jordan, the area of Edom, will experience the judgment of destruction. This will be a destruction with dead bodies covering the mountains, hills, and valleys (Ezek. 35:6-9).

Jeremiah 49:7-13 tells us:

Concerning Edom, thus saith the LORD of hosts; Is wisdom no more in Teman? is counsel perished from the prudent? is their wisdom vanished? Flee ye, turn back, dwell deep, O inhabitants of Dedan; for I will bring the calamity of Esau upon him, the time that I will visit him. If grapegatherers come to thee, would they not leave some gleaning grapes? if thieves by night, they will destroy till they have enough. But I have made Esau bare, I have uncovered his secret places, and he shall not be able to hide himself: his seed is spoiled, and his brethren, and his neighbours, and he is not. Leave thy fatherless children, I will preserve them alive; and let thy widows trust in me. For thus saith the LORD; Behold, they whose judgment was not to drink of the cup have assuredly drunken; and art thou he that shall altogether go unpunished? thou shalt not go unpunished, but thou shalt surely drink of it. For I have sworn by myself, saith the LORD, that Bozrah shall become a desolation, a reproach, a waste, and a curse; and all the cities thereof shall be perpetual wastes.

In these passages, there is the totality of Edom's destruction. The seed of Edom is destroyed (verses 7-10), and Edom is given the opportunity to trust in the Lord, but would not respond (verse 11). So, the cup of iniquity is poured out on the country of Edom and they must drink of God's wrath (verse 12). As a result, the land of Edom becomes an astonishment, a reproach, a waste, and a curse (verse 13). This destruction of Edom comes by means of war and conflict (Jer. 49:19-20). This is further explained in the prophecy of Obadiah.

Here, the prophet Obadiah tells us that Edom will not be helped by her friends or by their own wisdom or military forces (Obadiah 1:7-9). This destruction will come at the time of Israel's restoration (Obadiah 1:17), meaning at the time of Armageddon. The destruction of Edom is brought about by Israel (Obadiah 1:18). Perhaps this destruction is brought about by her army or the Israeli Defense Forces, mentioned so often by so many other commentators.

Here, Edom is described as stubble and kindling that will easily catch fire while Israel is the flame and fire that destroys. This fire destroys the descendants of Edom while Jacob's descendants possess the mountains of Edom and the destruction of Edom will fall from the mountain of Zion (Obadiah 1:19-21; Ezek. 25:12-14). Only through total destruction will peace come between Israel and Edom.

Ancient Moab, or modern central Jordan will suffer destruction, but it will not be total but rather a partial destruction (Jer. 48:1-46). Nonetheless, a remnant will return to the Lord. *"Yet will I bring again the captivity of Moab in the latter days, saith the LORD. Thus far is the judgment of Moab"* (Jer. 48:47).

Ammon, or northern Jordan will also suffer partial destruction and become a possession of Israel, but there will also be a remnant saved of Ammon in northern Jordan. *"And afterward I will bring again the captivity of the children of Ammon, saith the LORD"* (Jer. 49:6).

Thus, there will be a total destruction of southern Jordan, and a partial destruction of central and northern Jordan, and a remnant of these people will be saved.

The Future of Egypt

Egypt has long been one of Israel's most hated enemies and foes. Peace will come between the two lands through destruction and conversion. In Isaiah 19:1-22, the future of Egypt is foretold. Because of her sins, Egypt is characterized by civil war, desolation, and famine. The root of their desolation is because of their evil leaders (verses 11-15).

The Egyptian attacks on Israel and their routing resulted in a fear of Israel from Egypt (verses 16-17). This has only been true since the four modern wars with Israel, especially the attack of 1967 with heavy Egyptian losses, and this fear of Israel continues even today.

Eventually, peace will come between the nations as Hebrew, the language of Canaan in Isaiah's day, will be spoken in five Egyptian cities (Isa. 19:18). These will apparently be Jewish-populated cities that will eventually bring conversion to the nation of Egypt (Isa. 19:19-22).

An altar to the Lord is built in the land (verse 20). Egypt will be oppressed by the Antichrist (Dan. 11:42-43) but God will save them from their oppressors (Isa. 19:20). Egypt will worship God with sacrifices and oblations (verse 21) and as they are regenerated, God will heal their land as they turn in faith to God (verse 22). However, because of Egypt's long history of hatred with Israel, they will suffer desolation and destruction similar to Edom. But because they turned to the Lord, this desolation will last only the first forty years of the Millennium (Ezek. 29:1–6).

When Egypt returns to the Lord in believing faith, peace will come between the nations, although Egypt will endure an extended forty years of judgment when the land is desolate. Then after the forty-year judgment, the land of Egypt will also be blessed and turn into a paradise similar to Israel.

The Future of Assyria (Iraq and Syria)

The land of ancient Assyria is today the same area as the countries of modern Iraq and Syria. Peace will come between these nations and Israel by conversion. Isaiah 19:23–25 says,

> *In that day shall there be a highway out of Egypt to Assyria, and the Assyrian shall come into Egypt, and the Egyptian into Assyria, and the Egyptians shall serve with the Assyrians. In that day shall Israel be the third with Egypt and with Assyria, even a blessing in the midst of the land: Whom the LORD of hosts shall bless, saying, Blessed be Egypt my people, and Assyria the work of my hands, and Israel mine inheritance.*

This section of Isaiah describes a future economic partnership of Israel with Egypt and Assyria. In ancient times, there was an ancient highway of trade, the *Via Maris*, that operated between these nations but ceased to function in 1948. But in the Millennium, this highway and trade between the nations will be restored.

Earlier, we saw the conversion of the Egyptians and this conversion will also include the Assyrians to become a blessing to the Earth and to receive a blessing from God. The conclusion of Isaiah 19 shows there is economic and political unity between the nations because God proclaims Egypt will be my people, Assyria the work of my hands, and Israel my inheritance. This unity and peace come because they all worship the Lord and so there can be peace among the nations.

The Future of Kedar and Hazor (Saudi Arabia)

The earlier areas of Kedar and Hazor are currently modern Saudi Arabia. Peace will come with the destruction of Saudi Arabia through war. This will cause total devastation to the country and the people will be scattered and dispersed throughout the world.

Jeremiah 49:33 says, *"And Hazor shall be a dwelling for dragons, and a desolation for ever: there shall no man abide there, nor any son of man dwell in it."*

Because of this war, Saudi Arabia will be a perpetual devastation throughout the entire Millennium. Egypt will suffer a short-term desolation of forty years, but the desolation of Saudi Arabia will last the entire thousand years. The extent of the desolation of Saudi Arabia is not known.

The Future of Elam (Persia or Iran)

The people of Persia and Iran are not actually Arab but are more closely related to the Aryan tribes of Central Asia which moved to the area of Iran. But because of their interaction with Israel and their connection to other Arab nations through their religion of Islam, their fate will be considered.

Peace will come between Iran and Israel through destruction (Jer. 49:34–39). The destruction of Iran will be partial and the dispersion of the people temporary. This destruction will cause the people of Elam (southwestern Iran) to be scattered all over the world, but the people of Iran will eventually return and resettle Iran.[102]

This judgment is also similar to the judgment of Egypt but the time of the disbursement and return of Elam is not given. This means there will again be a kingdom of Elam or Iran in the future Millennium and there must be a remnant from Elam or Iran that believe and return.

The Future of Babylon

The Bible tells us much about the future of Babylon in prophecy. Bible prophecy foretells of the future fall of Ecclesiastical Babylon (the one-world church or one-world religion — Rev. 17:16) and the later destruction of Political Babylon (the one-world government) during the Campaign of Armageddon (Zech. 5:5–11; Isa. 13:1–14; Jer. 50–51; Rev. 18).

Earlier, we have seen continual destruction and devastation in Saudi Arabia and Edom. The future of Babylon is also total devastation and destruction. The city of Babylon, the capital of Antichrist, is destroyed (Isa. 13:20–22). This complete destruction is compared to the earlier destruction by God of Sodom and Gomorrah (Jer. 50:39–40).

The destruction is so severe that no man will even pass through the land of Babylon (Jer. 51:41–43). Because of the continual burning of the land, nothing of this Earth can live there, including animals, but it becomes the residence of demons with continual smoke and burning (Isa. 13:22–23; Jer. 50:39–40; Rev. 18:1–2). These demons confined in Babylon have animal-like features and they are what is held in Babylon.

Like Babylon, Edom will also be a place of perpetual

---

102. Ibid, p. 353.

burning and a place of confinement for demons (Isa. 34:8–15). This place of burning pitch and burning brimstone will be inhabited by beings that look similar to wild birds and animals but are actually demons. This includes demons in goat form, night demons, and others.

Because of Edom's glee over the fall of Israel and Judah (Ezek. 35:10–13), she will also be judged like Sodom and Gomorrah (Jer. 49:17–18). While the entire Earth becomes a beautiful paradise, Edom will be a destruction (Ezek. 35:14).

The only areas of the world to never become a beautiful paradise in the Millennium are Saudi Arabia, Edom, and Babylon. However, Babylon and Edom are a continual place of burning fires of judgment and a dwelling and residence only of demons, so these nations are the most devastated by God's judgment.

Thus, Babylon and Edom are given extremely severe judgment and these nations have an especially grave future with destruction and devastation throughout the entire Millennial Kingdom.

The Conditions of the World in Millennial Peace

A new world order is truly coming and it is a world that surpasses description and defies imagination! Can you dream of living in a whole new world? Yet, what is this Millennial world like? The world will change in many ways and different spheres or areas, both physically and spiritually. Specifically, how will the world change?

Peace in the Animal World

Animals will no longer attack and fight each other and are apparently non-carnivorous as there is **peace between beast and beast.** They will not have the wild nature to attack humans or other animals and they will not eat other animals but will eat vegetation. As Isaiah 11:6–7 reveals:

"The wolf also shall dwell with the lamb, and the leopard shall lie down with the kid; and the calf and the young lion and the fatling together; and a little child shall lead them. And the cow and the bear shall feed; their young ones shall lie down together: and the lion shall eat straw like an ox."

Fear will no longer exist as there will be **peace between man and beast.** Mankind will not fear animals and animals will not fear man. God describes this amazing time:

"And in that day will I make a covenant for them with the beasts of the field, and with the fowls of heaven, and with the creeping things of the ground ..." (Hosea 2:18).

"And I will ... cause the evil beasts to cease out of the land: and they shall dwell safely in the wilderness, and sleep in the woods" (Ezekiel 34:25).

Even the serpent, earlier used by Satan to deceive Eve in the Garden of Eden and cursed by God, will no longer be poisonous and a feared danger. A very young, innocent child can play unattended and not be hurt by formerly dangerous snakes or deadly animals. Isaiah 11:8 says: *"And the sucking child shall play on the hole of the asp, and the weaned child shall put his hand on the cockatrice' den."* Man need not fear lions or snakes and sheep need not fear predators such as wolves. Children can play in perfect safety among the fiercest of beasts.

Peace in the Natural World

The field, cursed on account of man's sin, will no longer be cursed (Gen. 3:17; Rom. 8:20-21). The world will be transformed into a beautiful paradise as God blesses the vegetable world. Except in the places of continual judgment such as short-term judgment on Egypt and especially perpetual judgment in Babylon and Edom, all of the world will become inhabited with many areas of farming so plentiful that the reapers will follow the farmers as they sow the fields. The deserts and mountains will also become a paradise of wonder.

Canaan, the ancient name of the land of Israel, will be especially blessed as a land that flows with milk and honey (Joel 3:18; Jer. 11:5), becoming a garden of paradise like Eden of old (Isa. 51:3; Ezek. 36:35), with flowering gardens, fruitful fields, mountains which run with corn, new oil and wine, with rain of blessing, with overflowing harvests, and with joy and delight in every plain, forest, and field (Amos 9:14; Ezek. 36:29–30; Joel 2:19; Ezek. 34:26; Lev. 26:5; Isa. 55:12).

As Isaiah 41:18 foretold: *"And I will open rivers in high places, and fountains in the midst of the valleys: I will make the wilderness a pool of water, and the dry land springs of water."*

The entire world will turn into a beautiful paradise and an ideal land of blessing, except for those few areas under judgment. Man will possess and inhabit a world of plenty with blessings in boundless food and all of his living needs met. There will be rejoicing of God as people sing His praises all the day long and delight in their daily blessings. This continual singing and rejoicing will be worldwide.

Peace in the Human World

In this new Millennial world, there will be no more war, no more striving for power or selfish gain, but in peace, all men will honor one another and serve Jesus as Lord and King (Isa. 2:4; 19:23; 66:23; Zech. 14:9). The human body will last naturally a thousand years and people will have vitality and vigor into old age.

People will be blessed with bodily health, profitable labor, social righteousness, mutual community assistance, God-determined borders, general disarmament, and God-determined equity of rights (Isa. 35:5–6; 65:20–23;

11:3-4; 58:7; 19:25; Acts 17:26; Mic. 4:3; Matt. 8:11; Zech. 2:11). Men will not fear for their safety from man or beast but they will have abundant food, live in absolute righteousness and equality, and have a blessed extended life, with many people on Earth living to the age of a thousand years old in their natural bodies.

Peace in the Spiritual World

At the commencement of this Theocratic Kingdom of Messiah, Satan will be bound and cast into a great abyss called "the bottomless pit" (Rev. 20:1-3). Evidently all demonic forces are restricted during this kingdom of righteousness.

Of the angelic creation, only God's divine, pure angels will dwell in the celestial heavens and minister His will on Earth. They will also help people on Earth as a part of God's Kingdom blessings.

Man Still Sins and Needs Salvation in the Millennium

Men will no longer be tempted and oppressed by demonic spirits during this period, nor by the world, but all sin will come from the hearts of unregenerate men alone and yet even during this wonderful period of righteousness, some men will not believe in Christ. Because man is born a fallen sinner in need of salvation, there will still be the need for personal salvation of every individual.

Salvation is always accomplished by having a new spiritual rebirth, being born again (John 3:3, 16). Salvation is not of works but only by receiving the grace of God (Eph. 2:8-9). Salvation is the gift of God that is received by repenting of your sins, believing on Jesus as your personal Savior, and accepting the gift of eternal life (Rom. 6:23).

Yet, there is also an unusual situation for salvation during the Millennium. Isaiah 65:20 says: *"There shall be no more thence an infant of days, nor an old man that hath not filled his days: for the child shall die an hundred years old; but the sinner being an hundred years old shall be accursed."*

This verse tells us that the life span of mankind has been increased beyond a hundred years (and it will be a thousand years or more), so people will live a long time and enjoy their extreme old age with energy and vigor, literally filling their days with renewed life.

The Lifespan Is Tied to Salvation in the Millennium

But the verse also tells us that when a person dies at a hundred years, it will seem as if a child has died, because it is so normal for a person to live a millennium that a hundred years is only the life span of a very young child. This verse also tells us that the person who died was cursed by God, so it seems that man has a hundred years to believe in God as their Savior and if they do not believe, then they will die.

While this may seem as if God was not merciful, God gives mankind life, especially extended at this time. In the Millennium, He gives mankind a hundred years to believe, while living in a world full of the witness of the Church Age saints, the witness of the Old Testament saints and the Tribulation saints, the lack of demonic temptation and oppression, and the ability to see and hear God Himself seated on His earthly throne. Yet, because of a sinful heart, some people will still choose not to believe in God.

The Challenge of Evil to Millennial Peace

Satan will be loosed for a season. Will this be the end of peace on Earth? Satan will be loosed out of the bottomless pit at the end of the Millennium to deceive the world. Revelation 20:7–9 tells us:

And when the thousand years are expired, Satan will be loosed out of his prison, And shall go out to deceive the nations which are in the four quarters of the earth, Gog and Magog, to gather them together to battle: the number of whom is as the sand of the sea. And they went up on the breadth of the earth, and compassed the camp of the saints about, and the beloved city: and fire came down from God out of heaven, and devoured them.

Here, we can see that when Satan is freed, he takes the opportunity to defy God and again to deceive and rule man.

Man Will Still Need to Give His Heart to God

Man is still sinful and, without Christ in his heart, he can be deceived. The Bible tells us about how vulnerable the heart is. Jeremiah 17:9 says, *"The heart is deceitful above all things, and desperately wicked: who can know it?"*

Even though man may think that he has control of his mind and heart, man is still a sinner and can be tempted to sin in his heart by his own flesh. 1 John 2:16 tells us, *"For all that is in the world, the lust of the flesh, and lust of the eyes, and the pride of life, is not of the Father, but is of the world."*

Without temptation from outside sources, such as temptation from sinful acquaintances, family, or friends, mankind has to fight an inner battle of temptation from things that attack his mind and heart. These are things that are attractive to mankind and cause lust of the flesh, things that we see, covet, and lust with our eyes, and things that we desire out of our will and prideful self, such as the pride of life.

As a result of this internal fighting and temptation, man will sin. Even in a perfect world without outside temptation and temptation from demons or the devil, man is born a sinner, and man will sin and need a Savior.

Satan Will Lead People to Reject God and Follow Him

Although God has personally reigned with man for these thousand years, some people will be deluded into denying Christ and apparently millions of people join forces with Satan as he invades to attack Jerusalem, the City of God, and leads his final attempt to overthrow God in this later Gog and Magog rebellion.

By this time in Earth's future, it is estimated that the Millennium would begin with 4 billion people on Earth. With the presence of no wars, no illness, and death almost unknown as people continue to populate the world, it is conservatively estimated that the world's population would have grown to at least 50 billion people.

After his release from the bottomless pit, Satan goes throughout the people and deceives many people who have not yet believed. Because all unbelievers will die if not saved by the age of one hundred, then this would be people from earlier ages who are less than a hundred years old, or essentially a rebellion of a youth movement.

Yet, this deception by Satan is so encompassing that when the rebellious force of unbelievers invades Israel to come to Jerusalem ("the beloved city") it is a mass of humanity so large that it looks like the sand of the sea. This rebellious force could easily be several hundred million or even a billion people.

Jesus Will Bring the Final End of Rebellion and Satan's Work

As a response, God does not fear Satan at the gates, nor does He lead an army to overthrow this final rebellion for now the Prince of Peace reigns on Earth. No human force on Earth and no supernatural angelic force of the heavens can threaten this peace. Remember that Christ has already defeated the combined armies of this Earth at Armageddon. He can just speak His word and create, and He can speak His word and destroy. God is the victor over sin, death, Hell, and the grave, and He can overcome any force of mankind or any rebellion by Satan and his forces.

Christ simply calls fire down from Heaven to destroy this vast army of unbelievers and then casts Satan into the lake of fire. This is the final chapter on Satan's impact and influence on rebellion in the world. Christ has finally overcome Satan and put his head under Christ's foot, as prophesied in Genesis 3:15. Christ is the victor over all evil, and He is the victor over Satan as He promised.

This event is a similar situation to the earlier Gog and Magog war because of the similarity of multiple armies coming to attack the nation of Israel. In the earlier Gog and Magog war, the invaders looked like a cloud that covered the land. Now, the invading people are so numerous as to look like the sands of the sea. That is probably why the name of the rebellion is called Gog and Magog. It is often called the Gog and Magog Rebellion or Gog and Magog II. Yet, this is not actually a war but rather a final rebellion and is distinct from the earlier Gog and Magog war in many ways.

In the earlier war, the invaders and protesters are mentioned as nations. In this rebellion, there are no invading nations, but deceived and rebellious people. In the early Magog war, they were led by Gog. In this rebellion, they are led by Satan. In the earlier conflict, they buried the dead for seven months and burned the weapons for seven years. In this conflict, all invaders are destroyed with fire from Heaven. Thus, they are separated by one thousand and seven years and are distinct conflicts.

Peace Eternal with the Triune God

After the final rebellion of the second Gog and Magog conflict, God will destroy this world with fervent heat, melt the elements, and then remake the Earth. In Colossians 1:17, it tells us that God holds the elements together. He will just let go of the elements, and the world will be immediately destroyed. At this time, there will be a great noise heard throughout the universe as God destroys this world and the entire region of outer space. Then God will build it back again as a New Earth, and a New Heaven.

This new Heaven will include a new Earth, a new city of God, and a new universe. The Holy City, fifteen hundred miles square, will descend and sit upon the Earth, and there all believers will live and serve the Lord forever in eternity future. In this new world of eternal Heaven on Earth, gone is all sickness and death, gone is all sin with its consequences, and gone are all tears and unhappiness. There will never again be jealousy or fighting, misunderstandings, pride, or any other conflict, but only a future eternal order with God in perfect serenity.

This new life in a new Heaven and Earth will be eternal peace with the Father, the Son, and the Holy Spirit, the Triune God, where we will live in perfect peace, love, and harmony with God Himself! It will be a whole new world.

EPILOGUE

God had promised Israel that he would make an everlasting covenant of peace with them that would bring eternal peace to Earth, and God's Word is sure (Ezek. 37:26). Men today seek peace in military maneuvers, diplomatic negotiations, and even through monetary means. But real lasting peace is only found in Jesus. Only Jesus can bring peace to the world and only by knowing Jesus as Savior can you have peace for your soul. Have you found that true peace? Have you believed in Jesus as your Savior?

Pure Peace for Believers Is Possessed Through the Imminent Rapture

It is wonderful to have real peace in this world and hope for the future. But without God, there is no peace or hope. Romans 15:13 says: *"Now the God of hope fill you with all joy and peace in believing, that ye may abound in hope, through the power of the Holy Ghost."*

There is peace today for believers in Jesus. They have daily peace to weather the storms of life with a "peace that passeth all understanding." Believers have peace in their hearts, not because of their inherent strength, but because of their faith in God. Believers can face enormous difficulties and even death with quiet confidence that baffles the world. They can also face an uncertain future by knowing of the hope of the Second Coming of Jesus. While the future looks bleak and without any hope of peace or happiness, the believer can be full of peace.

The Bible tells of a future that is more evil, and full of death, devastation, and woe, than all of man's earlier existence, and this is the time of the coming Tribulation.

However, before the commencement of the Tribulation period, the most devastating time of God's judgment on Earth, the coming of Jesus for his saints in the Rapture will occur (1 Thess. 4:13–18; 5:9; Rev. 3:10).

The Redeemed of this world, those who have trusted Christ as Savior, are not appointed unto wrath but are kept from the hour of trial which shall come upon all the Earth. The Rapture will occur before the Russian invasion of Israel and before the rise of the Antichrist as a world leader.

What a thrill it is to know that Jesus is coming personally to take you to Heaven! You will not only escape the second death, but also the wrath of God in the Tribulation period, and instead experience His return, His rest, His righteousness, and His later reign. This is the "blessed hope" of the saints when Jesus shall return for His faultless Bride, shall give us the redemption of the fallen body, and shall reward the faithful believers. Forever you shall expound His promises, exemplify His plan, explore His Kingdom, and experience His presence.

Are you ready for Christ's soon return in the Rapture? Have you trusted Jesus as your only way of salvation?

Personal Peace Is Offered to the World Today Through Jesus

Today, the genuine source of peace is the inner peace of personal salvation. Jesus tells us, "... *my peace I give unto you: not as the world giveth, give I unto you* ..." (John 14:27).

Only by repenting of your sin and believing on Jesus Christ as the only true Savior can you free yourself of enmity with God and find real and lasting *"peace with God"* (Rom. 5:1). This spiritual peace is promised to all who believe that Jesus is God manifest in the flesh, who died in the sinner's place on the cross and was resurrected the third day, so that the believer may receive forgiveness and eternal life (Acts 16:31; Rom. 5:8-10; Col. 1:20).

Yes, you can find real peace for your soul. Will you believe in Jesus today as your personal Savior?

The Way to Eternal Life and Peace Is Through Jesus Christ

You may wonder, How can I know this real peace and find the way to eternal life? The way to eternal life is only through Jesus Christ. In John 14:6, Jesus said, *"... I am the way, the truth and the life: no man cometh to the Father, but by me."*

Realize that Jesus is the only way to eternal life in Heaven. He and He alone can save you and He alone is the way to Heaven. Romans 3:10 says, *"... There is none righteous, no, not one."* And Romans 3:23 adds, *"For all have sinned and come short of the glory of God."*

Realize that you are a sinner who has sinned against God and you cannot make it to Heaven in your sinful condition. This is because all people are sinners. Romans 6:23 tells us, *"For the wages of sin is death; but the gift of God is eternal life through Jesus Christ, our Lord."*

Because of our sins, we must face God in personal judgment. All of our sins must be paid for, and the only payment mankind can offer for their sin is to die and suffer eternally in the fires of Hell. Good works cannot save us or pay for our sins. There is nothing we can do on Earth to pay for our sins but face God in judgment.

But Jesus loved us and He made a way to escape eternal death in Hell for our sins. Instead, He came to pay for our sins by dying for us on the cross. Jesus, as the sinless Son of God, died for the sins of the world and His death and payment for sin can be applied to us because he died for us.

Romans 5:8 says, *"But God commendeth his love toward us, in that, while we were yet sinners, Christ died for us."*

Jesus so loved the entire world that he came to provide and offer salvation to the world. By believing in Him, you can have eternal life. John 3:16 says, *"For God so loved the world, that he gave his only begotten Son, that whosoever believeth in him should not perish, but have everlasting life."*

Jesus came to offer salvation to anyone who would repent of their sin and believe in Him as their personal savior. He offers the gift of eternal life freely to anyone who will call upon the Lord to save him. Romans 10:9–10 says: *"That if thou shalt confess with thy mouth the Lord Jesus, and shalt believe in thine heart that God hath raised him from the dead, thou shalt be saved. For with the heart man believeth unto righteousness; and with the mouth confession is made unto salvation."*

This means you must understand the way to Heaven and personally believe in Jesus. Also, you must call unto the Lord in a prayer of salvation to God. Romans 10:13 tells us, *"For whosoever shall call upon the name of the Lord shall be saved."*

Would you like to be saved today and to know that one day Heaven will be your home? Just call upon Jesus today to save you now. You can pray:

Dear Lord,

I know that I am a sinner and that I have sinned against God. But I want to turn from my sin and believe in you as my personal Savior. I believe that Jesus is the Son of God who died on the cross for my sins and rose on the third day, proving that He is God. I ask you now to save me from Hell and give me eternal life and a home in Heaven. In Jesus' name, Amen.

If you prayed to believe in Jesus and to save you and to take you to Heaven, we can be assured that Jesus saved you the moment you prayed and believed. That means we have the assurance that Heaven will be our eternal home, no matter what happens in the future.

After you have trusted in Christ, try to read the Bible, starting in the New Testament, to learn more about Jesus and your new faith. You can talk to God daily in prayer and begin to live for God as a believer. Also, please tell others about your new faith in Jesus and find a good Bible-believing and Bible-teaching church where you can learn more about the Bible and your new faith in God.

John 10:28 assures us that we can never lose our salvation or eternal life. Jesus says, *"And I give unto them eternal life; and they shall never perish, neither shall any man pluck them out of my hand."*

Thus, we can know that we are saved forever and know that one day we will be in Heaven. And 1 Peter 1:5 says, we are *"... kept by the power of God through faith unto salvation, ..."* meaning God keeps us saved. We cannot earn salvation by any works of our own, and when we receive Christ, we cannot lose salvation because God keeps us saved. We do not do good works to keep ourselves saved but we are kept saved eternally by the power of God alone.

In these last days, be encouraged that Jesus is coming soon to defeat evil, Satan, the Antichrist, and his forces, and Jesus will set up his Millennial reign on Earth. The wars of this world may come, but in the end, Jesus will overcome all war and all evil and bring peace to the world.

He will rule the world in a new kind of existence without the worry of fighting and war. When Jesus comes, it will be *"Peace on earth, good will toward men."* How exciting it is for the believer to not worry or fret, and to have peace and hope in all things because Jesus is coming again!

For any questions or comments, please contact
Dr. Lonnie Shipman
103 Bleriot Place
Grand Prairie, Texas 75051
lonnie@lonnieshipman.com

BIBLIOGRAPHY

Bultema, Harry, *Commentary on Isaiah,* (Grand Rapids: Kregel Publishers, 1981).

Couch, Mal, Gen. Ed. *The Dictionary of Premillennial Theology,* (Grand Rapids, MI: Kregel Press, 1995).

Falwell, Jerry, Exec. Ed., Hindson, Ed, Gen. Ed., *The Liberty Bible Commentary — Old Testament* (Nashville, TN: Thomas Nelson, 1982).

Feinberg, Charles L., "Jeremiah," *The Expositor's Bible Commentary,* Gen. Ed. Frank E. Gaebelein, Vol. 6 (Grand Rapids, MI: Zondervan, 1986).

Fruchtenbaum, Arnold, *Footsteps of the Messiah,* (Tustin, CA: Ariel Ministries Press, 1963).

----*Israelogy: The Missing Link in Systematic Theology,* (Tustin, CA: Ariel Ministries Press, 1989).

Gesenius, Wilhelm, *Gesenius' Hebrew and Chaldean Lexicon* (Grand Rapids: Eerdmans Publishing Company, 1949).

Goodman, Philip, *The Psalm 83 Prophecy,* (Tulsa, OK: Bible Prophecy as Written, Sept./Oct. 2013).

Hindson, Ed, LaHaye, Tim, *Global Warning: Are We on the Brink of World War III?* (Eugene, OR: Harvest House Publishers, 2008).

Hitchcock, Mark, *After the Empire,* (Wheaton, IL: Tyndale House Publishers, 1994).

----*Iran: The Coming Crises* (Sisters, OR: Multnomah, 2006).

----*Showdown with Iran,* (Emanate Books, 2020).

Ice, Thomas, *The Case for Zionism: Why Christians Should Support Israel,* (Green Forest, AR: New Leaf Press, 2017).

Keil, C.F., "Ezekiel, Daniel," *Commentary on the Old Testament,* trans. James Martin (Grand Rapids: Eerdmans Publishing Company, 1982).

Lindsey, Hal, *There's a New World Coming: A Prophetic Odyssey* (Irvine, CA: Harvest House Publishers, 1973).

Netanyahu, Benjamin, "Netanyahu's 2024 Address to Congress," *Ha'aretz*.

Phillips, John, *Exploring the Future*, (Kregel Publications, 2003).

Price, Randall, *Fast Facts on the Middle East*, (Eugene, OR: Harvest House Publishers, 2003).

----Gen. Ed., *What Should We Think About Israel? Separating Facts from Fiction in the Middle East Conflict*, (Eugene, OR: Harvest House Publishers, 2019).

Reagan, David, *9 Wars of the End Times*, (McKinney, TX: Lamb & Lion Ministries, 2023).

Rosenberg, Joel C., *Epicenter: Why the Current Rumblings in the Middle East Will Change Your Future*, (Carol Stream, IL: Tyndale, 2000).

Salus, Bill, *Nuclear Showdown in Iran: Revealing the Ancient Prophecy of Elam*, (Las Quinta, CA: Prophecy Depot Ministries, 2014).

Scroggie, William, *The Unfolding Drama of Redemption*, (Kregel Classics, 1995).

Walvoord, John F., *Every Prophecy of the Bible*, (Colorado Springs, CO: Chariot Victor Publishing, 1999).

Willmington, Harold L., *Willmington's Guide to the Bible*, (Tyndale House Publishers, 2011).

Yamauchi, Edwin M., *Foes from the Northern Frontier*, (Grand Rapids: Baker Book House, 1982).

ABOUT THE AUTHOR

Dr. Lonnie Shipman

Traveling in a worldwide ministry as an evangelist and concert pianist, Lonnie Shipman was born into a preacher's family and saved at age six. Trained as a concert pianist, he won six national piano competitions and toured forty-eight states and Canada as a teenager. After being called to preach at age fifteen, Lonnie graduated from high school as valedictorian and entered Bible college.

A product of a musical family that has toured nationally, Lonnie Shipman is dedicated to reaching souls with the Gospel of Christ. He travels throughout America and the world preaching the Gospel, performing concerts, teaching in colleges, and giving prophetic, biblical, archaeological, and biblical heritage conferences and music seminars.

As his testimony acclaims, *"My consuming desire is to see a Heaven-sent revival that will reach the lost and awake the church to a total commitment to Jesus. There is nothing more important than winning souls to Christ."*

An author, Dr. Shipman's writings give insight into biblical, prophetic, musical, archaeological, and historical subjects and include on-location photographs of biblical places, original prophecy charts, and biblical maps.

When first led to enter evangelism, Dr. Shipman felt burdened to travel throughout the world preaching the

Gospel to reach souls in the regions beyond. He has now preached in twenty-seven countries on thirty-one international tours.

He has preached and presented concerts in North America, including Canada, Mexico, and the continental forty-eight states, as well as South America, the Caribbean, the Middle East, and Eastern and Western Europe, appearing personally to over 10 million people and millions on television in America and Europe.

Dr. Shipman has preached with two prime ministers of Europe and has performed piano in many European concert halls, two royal palaces of Europe, Oxford University, and Madison Square Garden in New York.

In May 2003 and in May 2023, he presented prophecy studies at Louisiana Baptist Theological Seminary and Louisiana Baptist University, Shreveport, LA.

In May 2009, Dr. Shipman was a presenter at Piano Texas 2009, at Texas Christian University, Fort Worth, Texas, along with professors from the Julliard School.

In March 2013, he was part of the Bible exposition at the Washington Capital Mall and participated in "The Significance of the 400th Anniversary of the King James Version of the Bible," at George Washington University, Georgetown, VA.

Lonnie Shipman has attended eleven colleges and graduated from Arlington Baptist University (B.S. in Bible), Dallas Baptist University (B.M. in Piano Performance and Violin), Baptist Christian College (B.A.), Louisiana Baptist University (M.A.), Baptist University of Florida (M.M. in Worship Leadership, with emphasis in Piano Performance and Sacred Music), Louisiana Baptist Theological Seminary (M.Div., Th. D. in Bible Prophecy), and Pacific International University (D.S.M. in Music Composition).

He has done graduate work at Pensacola Christian

College, Southwestern Baptist Theological Seminary, and has done a special research study at Christ Church, Oxford University, Oxford, England.

Dr. Shipman has served on the faculty of the Norris Bible Baptist Seminary and the Texas Baptist Bible College and has presented master classes at Crown College, Powell, TN, and the Seminario Biblico Bautista of San Antonio, TX, as *well as appearing on TBN's Creation in the 21st Century.*

Currently, he travels as an evangelist and concert pianist speaking in churches, conferences, and with the Southwest Radio Ministries.

Dr. Shipman's books include *Secrets of Prophecy Revealed: Keys to Jesus' Second Coming, Heaven's Orchestra: The Stars Sing Praise to God, Treasure and the Coming Temple of God: Finding the Ark and the Ashes, King of Books: The Bible in Archaeology and History,* and *Israel in Crisis: Her Future Wars and Final Peace* as well as being a contributor to *The Dictionary of Premillennial Theology.*

His sacred piano recordings include *My Redeemer's Praise,* and *Seeing God's Glory,* as well as the vocal recordings of *The Revelation of Jesus Christ* and *Songs of the Faith.*